THE TOP
CONSULTANT

THE TOP
CONSULTANT

DEVELOPING YOUR SKILLS FOR
GREATER EFFECTIVENESS

CALVERT MARKHAM

**KOGAN
PAGE**

First published in 1993

Kogan Page Limited
120 Pentonville Road
London N1 9JN

British Library Cataloguing in Publication Data

A CIP record for this book is available from the British Library.

ISBN 0 7494 0397 7

Typeset by DP Photosetting, Aylesbury, Bucks
Printed and bound in Great Britain by
Clays Ltd, St Ives plc

CONTENTS

ACKNOWLEDGEMENTS

This book is based on my experience in working with clients and fellow consultants. Much of my time has been spent in training consultants, and the learning has been a two-way process. I am grateful, therefore, for the comments, ideas and suggestions that I have had from the many participants in the training courses that I have run. Thanks are also due to the Institute of Management Consultants for permission to print the extracts from various codes and guidelines, that appear in the book.

I am grateful for the comments of friends involved with the consultancy profession who were able to make helpful comments on various parts of the book, particularly Graham Benjamin, Alan Elliot, Michael Grunberg, Mike Kearsley, and Professor Allan Williams. A particular debt of thanks is owed to Anthony Macdonald Smith for reading the whole book in draft and for his helpful comments.

Needless to say, however, I must take full responsibility for what appears herein.

Calvert Markham
November, 1992

9

INTRODUCTION

One of my first assignments as a management consultant was with one of the London teaching hospitals. I heard that a colleague was a patient in one of the wards, and I wanted to know which one, so I phoned the appropriate department. Information was given only reluctantly over the phone, and I was asked who I was. 'I'm a consultant and she's a member of my firm,' I replied, honestly. There was a sound of clicking heels and coming to attention at the other end of the phone – and I got the information I wanted immediately. 'Consultant' and 'firm' have quite different (and more potent) meanings in a hospital.

The term 'consultant' is now used for a variety of occupations; as well as the senior doctor and the management consultant, it is used to describe anybody who is providing knowledge-based services to an organisation on a contractual basis. So 'consultant' can also include solicitor, accountant, architect, engineer or, indeed, any professional.

Increasingly, organisations are concentrating on managing their core businesses and bringing in peripheral services from outside. In future more people will be consultants and so will need consultancy skills.

There are three components to consultancy skills:

- The body of knowledge, skills and experience which the consultant has on offer. This might be civil engineering, tax law, software applications or whatever the consultant purports to be expert in.

- Experience or knowledge of the application of the specialist skill to a specific area. For example, this might be an industrial sector, a geographical area, or a particular type of problem.

- Consultancy skills, which enable the consultant to deliver his or her expertise within the client environment.

These three components are like the legs of a three-legged stool: all have to be present if a consultant is to carry out the role effectively. If one leg is missing, the stool is at best wobbly and at worst, falls over.

This book concentrates on the third component – the skills required to engage in consultancy, which are necessary irrespective of the specialist expertise of the individual or the area of its application.

I am a management consultant, and so if the book has a bias, it is towards this group. But in my work I have come across other constituencies who will find it of value, for example:

- technical specialists who are now having to provide their services on a consultancy basis, especially if setting up their own consultancy practice;

- career consultants and other professionals who are progressing to more senior positions in their practice (eg solicitors, accountants);

- organisations which are developing businesses based on consultancy.

In designing the structure of the book, I have tried to follow a logical sequence: having defined the structure of consultancy projects, I go on to marketing, selling and other commercial aspects, and management matters in consultancy. After chapters on problem solving and intervention, the book concludes with how to retain a client as a long term buyer of consultancy services from your practice.

The topics that I have chosen to include are ones that I have found to be of interest to those entering or engaging in consultancy. For some readers, the material will be new; for others, there may be much that is familiar. However, I hope that all readers will find find topics of interest and value herein.

1

THE STRUCTURE OF CONSULTANCY PROJECTS

In Windsor Great Park there is a path – or, more accurately, an avenue – called the Long Walk. Extending for three miles in a straight line, it passes through the park towards Windsor Castle. The path is wide – you can wander within its limits, but its boundaries are clear – and, as you walk along it, the prospect of the Castle is always in view.

Some consultancy projects are like that path and are conducted by using an approach which is called a 'royal road' (no pun intended). From start to finish the path – the series of tasks required to conduct the project – is clear. There may be minor deviations along the way, but these will be within the broad boundaries. The outcome will be as clearly in sight as Windsor Castle.

By contrast, there are other consultancy projects that are forays into unknown territory. Like the search for El Dorado, these projects seek a goal that is believed to exist but whose detailed nature and location, and the path there, are uncertain. Such projects are needed when 'messy' or 'wicked' problems have to be addressed. As with a journey into the unknown, it is easy on these projects to lose your way; to take wrong turnings; to waste time; to fail to achieve the goal. But first you must recognise that you have to deal with a messy problem. The consultant unaware of this is like the young army officer whose colonel wrote of him, 'Undoubtedly there are soldiers who would follow this officer but, if so, it would be only out of a sense of curiosity to find out where he was going.'

One of the first things I do when teaching a course in consultancy is to invite participants to define consultancy. We usually arrive at a list of attributes, but rarely a coherent definition. Often the participants have been practising – successfully – as consultants for some years, so it is curious that they cannot rattle off their working definition. It is difficult because consultancy is a process that covers a broad spectrum of activity. Specialists in IT, manufacturing, marketing, corporate strategy design and recruitment can all describe themselves as consultants. Their approaches to consultancy projects may be different, so what unites them?

In this chapter we will examine the structure of consultancy projects. The differences in approach between various specialists will be seen to be the consequence of the different types of problems that they need to address, and so we start by considering the variety of consultancy problems, and the effect of these in influencing the level at which a consultant intervenes in a client organisation. Despite these differences, however, we shall see that consultants engage in similar activities on a project, whatever their specialisation.

THE VARIETY OF CONSULTANCY PROBLEMS

Consultancy problems fall on a spectrum, as shown in Figure 1.1.

At one end of the spectrum is technical consultancy; at the other, strategic; and, in between, functional consultancy. Technical consultancy is not confined to technology, but also includes consultancy that is carried out by specialists applying standard techniques, for example:

- a recruitment consultant, finding a suitable candidate to fill a job vacancy;

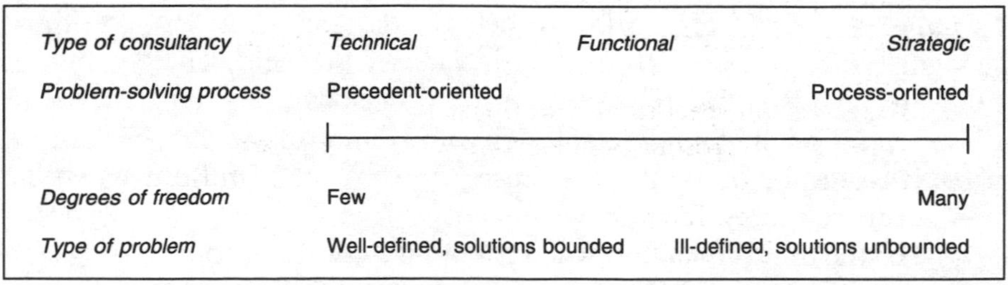

Type of consultancy	Technical	Functional	Strategic
Problem-solving process	Precedent-oriented		Process-oriented
	├───┤		
Degrees of freedom	Few		Many
Type of problem	Well-defined, solutions bounded	Ill-defined, solutions unbounded	

Figure 1.1 *The spectrum of consultancy*

14

- an accountant advising on a company's tax affairs;

- an IT consultant, advising on the choice of computer system.

In each of these cases, you may be working from precedent and be retained because of your knowledge. As a recruitment consultant, for example, you can rely on precedent; you will have had previous experience in identifying suitable job candidates for a vacant position. There is a royal road – a standard approach – that you can follow in carrying out a recruitment assignment, which is illustrated in Table 1.1.

By contrast, strategic consultancy is less likely to be based on precedent; the issues that have to be addressed in determining how a business is to develop and how it should be organised so to do will be unique to that business and its current circumstances.

Strategic consultancy involves more degrees of freedom than technical consultancy, and so precedent is less helpful. What is needed is a problem-solving process that can resolve ill-defined problems with unbounded solutions, rather than a 'royal road'. (Such a process is explained in Chapter 7.)

Between strategic and technical consultancy lies functional consultancy. Whereas strategic consultancy is concerned with a business as a whole, functional consultancy deals with the business on an aspect-by-aspect basis. This is the traditional province of management consultants, who might specialise in marketing, manufacturing,

Table 1.1 *Royal road for carrying out a recruitment assignment*

1. Get job description for new position
2. Identify key aspects of business and environment in which the new appointee will be working
3. Determine contents of remuneration package and scope for negotiation
4. Agree person specification with client
5. Agree an advertising campaign and copy to be used
6. Place adverts
7. Sort responses. Identify long list for interview
8. Interview and identify suitable candidates
9. Provide client with shortlist of names and reports on each

financial management, and so on. There is no watertight boundary between functional consultancy and its two neighbours. Functional consultancy can become involved with strategic concerns, and vice versa. Similarly, the implementation of functional consultancy can develop into technical consultancy.

At the technical end of the spectrum, therefore, problems are better defined and the form of the solution is (usually) predictable. In the examples given above, the recruitment consultant has to put forward suitable candidates; the client is unlikely to expect the recruitment consultant to come up with recommendations on – say – marketing and distribution policy. Similarly, the tax accountant has to recommend suitable accounting policies and the IT consultant will be expected to advise on the choice of computer system.

Conversely, at the strategic end of the spectrum, the problem(s) may initially be very poorly defined and much of the consultant's effort may be devoted to defining what the problem is in the first place. The consultant will spend a lot of time identifying salient features of the client's business and the environment in which it is conducted in order to identify the issues that need to be addressed in the first place. Recommendations will be less bounded, too, than those in functional consultancy; they may involve diversification or withdrawal from businesses, accessing new markets, developing or dropping products, and so on. The nature of the solutions is not necessarily known at the start. Functional consultancy may then be required when putting the strategic choices into practice.

WHERE DO YOU START A CONSULTANCY PROJECT?

Of course, technical consultants will seek to reassure themselves of the soundness of the assumptions underpinning their project. Thus, in the examples above:

- A recruitment consultant will want to understand the current operations of a business and how it is likely to develop, before advising on the recruitment of a senior executive.

- An accountant will need to understand the corporate structure and how it might change, before advising on optimising tax.

- An IT consultant will need to know how the DP requirements of a business are likely to develop before advising on the choice of computer.

If a client cannot provide satisfactory answers to these questions, then there may be functional or strategic consultancy work that needs to be done before a project in a technical area can proceed. Sometimes consultants are accused of commercial opportunism, setting out to enlarge the scope of their projects beyond the limits set by clients, when in fact extra work is necessary to provide a sufficiently sound basis for the original project to proceed. Indeed, it is usually good practice for a consultant to be at least thinking, if not working, at a degree of freedom beyond that set by the client's thinking.

> For example, a multinational firm was considering reviewing the remuneration packages of its top 200 or so executives. Some worked in subsidiary companies and some at head office, but for remuneration purposes all were treated as a single executive cadre. The consultant looked into the business and personnel policies used by the client and discovered that:
>
> - only rarely did an executive move from one subsidiary to another;
>
> - the subsidiaries were largely autonomous – they did not depend on one another.
>
> The executive cadre was a myth – there was no need for it. Thereafter, each executive was dealt with according to the subsidiary he or she worked for – the only 'executive cadre' was at corporate headquarters. The consultant had – necessarily – extended the scope of the brief to include issues of personnel policy so as to deal with the remuneration review satisfactorily.

This example illustrates the value of thinking at a degree of freedom greater than that of the client. What is therefore needed is a framework that allows a consultant to judge:

- how a client construes a problem;

- what constitutes 'thinking at a degree of freedom greater than the client'.

Different levels of intervention

The example above shows that there are different levels at which you can start a consultancy project. Where you start depends on your view of the nature of the problem to be dealt with; but first, it is essential to recognise that there are different levels of intervention in consultancy problem solving.

Table 1.2 shows the different levels at which a consultant can make an intervention. Although four levels are shown, they are on a continuum. For example, an issue can be thought of as a loosely defined problem – the more precisely a problem is defined and understood, the closer you get to a solution.

Each level proceeds on the basis of assumptions about the earlier level; for example, if your level of intervention is about formulating solutions, then this will be predicated on assumptions about the nature of the issues that have to be addressed. Similarly, the definition of issues will follow assumptions about purposes – what is to be achieved in the first place.

Table 1.2 *Levels of intervention*

1.	*Purposes*	The aims that the client has in mind when inviting consultancy help
2.	*Issues*	The problem areas that must be addressed if the purposes are to be achieved
3.	*Solutions*	What the solutions should be
4.	*Implementation*	The plans and activities for resolving the problem by means of the chosen solutions

The idea behind Table 1.2 can be illustrated by a simple case study – International Cutlery Company (ICC), which is set out below.

John Smith, a consultant, had been invited by the general manager of the International Cutlery Company to tender for a project with the aim of reducing the cost of producing cutlery. 'Our competitors seem to be able to produce it for a lot less than we can – and I want to get our costs down to the same level as theirs,' the general manager explained when Smith met him.

The business was a small subsidiary of Armfather Industries. As he showed Smith round the factory, the general manager explained what was going on. In one corner, a group of operatives were sitting around laughing and chatting. The general manager explained, 'They work on the "C" production line; they're having to wait whilst an engineer fixes the packaging machine.'

Quality control was very interesting; a large number of pieces of cutlery that did not meet specification had been placed in two piles. 'One pile are those which can easily be put right,' explained the quality inspector. 'Those others are a dead loss – they could never be fixed.' Smith asked whether the rejects were the result of the week's production so far. 'Goodness, no,' exclaimed the inspector. 'These are just this morning's.'

The general manager grumbled as they left. 'That means more overtime. Overtime costs are high enough as it is!'

Just as they reached the finishing shop, the general manager's secretary rushed up to them. 'I'm so glad to have caught you,' she said to him. 'Robinsons are on the line; they want to fix lunch sometime so that they can go over next year's prices with you.'

'I'd better talk to them,' said the general manager 'Can you excuse me whilst I pop back to my office for five minutes? Robinsons are our major suppliers,' he went on to explain, before he left. 'They produce first-class stuff, and their deliveries are always spot on. But they really charge for it! That meeting is to discuss the price increase they're proposing for next year.'

John Smith went on into the finishing shop with the supervisor who had been hovering in the background since he had walked in with the general manager. They had chatted about the different qualities of finish various customers required. One interesting thing he learned was that most of the specifications had not changed at all over the last five years.

With this background, John Smith might intervene at any of the four levels.

After the visit, the general manager (GM) of ICC might call up John Smith saying, 'As you can see, our main problem is the "C" production line. We obviously need to refurbish the equipment, and we'd like you to oversee the project.' A level 4 intervention would be for John Smith to implement the GM's plans and support the refurbishment.

At a level 3 intervention, John Smith would accept the GM's diagnosis of the problem, but might question the solution. He might look for other ways of improving the productivity on the 'C' production line – for example, by improved methods, materials flow or planning.

If John Smith intervened at level 2, he might identify other issues that could contribute to high production costs, besides those of the 'C' production line. During his visit, he might note:

- operatives idle while the packaging machine was being fixed;
- large piles of rejects;
- high overtime costs;
- high supplier prices;
- unchanged specifications.

He would need to check whether these are important contributory factors to high production costs; there may be other issues too, which need consideration.

Finally, if John Smith made a level 1 intervention, he would query the general manager's initial statement of purpose. Is it true that the production costs of his competitors are less? Does the financial structure of the cutlery business mean that ICC can match their competitors? Would it be worthwhile? These are all questions he might ask at this level.

Having identified the levels of intervention John Smith could make, you can see that the intervention at level 4 cited first is based on assumptions about the preceeding levels, namely that:

- ICC's competitors have a cost advantage and ICC must reduce production costs ; (level 1)
- improving performance on the 'C' production line will have a worthwhile impact on productivity; (level 2)
- refurbishing the machinery will improve productivity on the 'C' production line; (level 3)
- so implementing the GM's refurbishment plans will make ICC more competitive; (level 4).

Choosing where to start

All consultants should be aware of this hierarchy of intervention. Part of your expertise should be to judge at which level of intervention it is necessary to start and to guide your clients accordingly.

At the start of any involvement with a client (ie *before* a project has been defined) you must therefore ask the question:

> Can I take as read any assumptions about the levels above that at which I am operating, on which my work is predicated? Or is there a piece of work that needs to be done to check these out before I engage in the main piece of work?

Thinking at a degree of freedom more than that of the client means questioning the assumptions on which a client's construction of any problem is based. For example, a large company decided to make its IT department perform better, by insisting that it dealt with all internal 'customers' on a commercial basis. Other departments would then be free to use other sources of IT services if they could be provided more cheaply.

The manager of the IT department had considerable misgivings about this. Although there would be short-term cost savings, she believed that in the long term the quality of IT systems and support would fall. She decided to proceed with implementing this proposal, however, and discussed how it might be best accomplished with an outside consultant.

The consultant had at this point to choose at what level to intervene. A level 4 intervention would have meant setting up the IT department so that it could function effectively on a commercial basis. With a level 3 intervention (a degree of freedom greater than the client is thinking) the consultant would have looked at other ways in which the IT department could improve its service to other parts of the organisation.

In the event, on probing from the consultant, the manager disclosed her misgivings about this solution. Further probing revealed that the problem was really that internal departments resented the way that IT was costed into their budgets – as an overhead, rather than for services received. This meant that alternative solutions – changing the costing system – became more appropriate, and this was the solution eventually adopted.

Dealing with clients on these matters has to be handled sensitively to avoid appearing to be extending the scope of an assignment needlessly. On the domestic front, we do not welcome our plumber's help on matters other than plumbing – his advice on our financial affairs, for example, would be intrusive. Similarly, a client may become irritated with a training consultant who tries needlessly to develop a training assignment into matters of corporate strategy. Where a problem is clearly and satisfactorily defined, intervening at level 3, to define solutions, is entirely proper.

Of course, you may well have biases or preferences about where you start on a project. This will be strongly influenced by the type of consultancy in which you specialise. For example:

- A strategy or a process consultant may always start by questioning the purposes of a client (level 1).

- A management consultant may focus on identifying issues (level 2) and recommending how they might be resolved (level 3).

- A technical consultant will help with the implementation of a project (level 4).

It is important to recognise these biases, because you may be required to work at different levels. For example, an IT consultant may need to clarify issues in order to do the job. Similarly, a strategy consultant may need to follow a project through to detailed implementation.

PHASING

If you start a project with a level 4 intervention, then you can predict with a fair degree of confidence how the project will develop.

By contrast, with a level 1 intervention, it is more difficult to predict what will happen, as work at subsequent levels will depend on the findings of those preceding. Under these circumstances an iterative approach is appropriate, which breaks the consultancy project down into phases, as shown in Figure 1.2.

The work at each level is best dealt with as a separate phase in a project. This implies that in carrying a project through from clarifying purposes to implementing solutions, there should be at least four phases. If you start at level 3, however, you could manage with just two phases. Each phase, of course, could itself be a project with several stages involved.

The example of ICC can be used to illustrate phasing, as follows:

The GM telephones John Smith to say that he's concerned about the competitiveness of ICC, and he believes that production costs need to be reduced. John Smith visits the factory; his visit is reported in the account given earlier in this chapter. Based on his appraisal, John Smith accepts

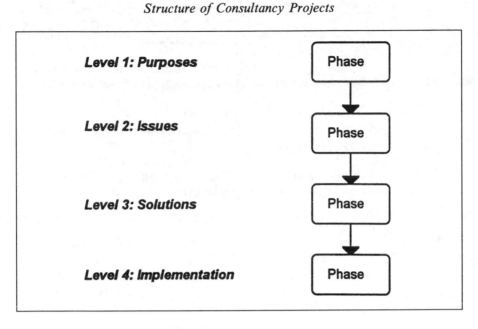

Figure 1.2 *Successive levels of intervention should be treated as different phases in a consultancy project*

the GM's view of the aims, and decides to start with a level 2 intervention – identifying the issues which lead to high production costs.

At the end of this phase, John Smith might report to the GM with his appraisal of the issues that must be addressed if ICC's production costs are to be reduced. The GM might then ask, 'What should we do to resolve these issues?'

This is a level 3 intervention, which therefore forms the next phase of the project. When this is complete, John Smith would report to the GM with recommendations on how the issues should be addressed. Finally, the GM might ask John Smith to implement his solutions (a level 4 intervention).

THE ACTIVITIES IN A CONSULTANCY PROJECT

Irrespective of the level of intervention or the number of phases in a consultancy project, however, you will find that consultants engage in similar activities in all their projects.

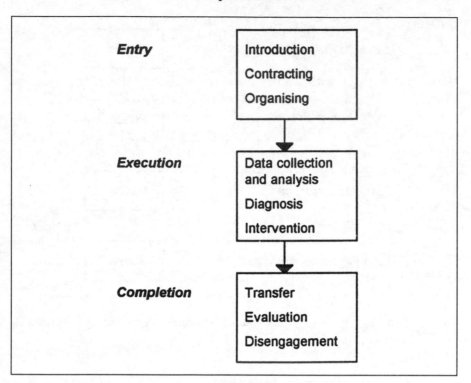

Figure 1.3 *Activities in a consultancy project*

The activities in a consultancy project can be broken down into three major stages as shown in Figure 1.3.

The three major stages are defined as follows:

- *Entry* is the work required at the start of a project.

- *Execution* is carrying out the project.

- *Completion* covers the closure procedures on the project.

The steps shown in Figure 1.3 show a project perspective – the commercial aspects, such as selling the project or defining the terms of reference are not shown. (Chapters 2–5 deal with commercial aspects of consultancy.) The steps in each of these major stages are described below.

Entry

Introduction

Your first contact with a client may be in selling an assignment, or starting an assignment which has already been sold. In either case, careful preparation is required and you should aim to make a favourable impact. There is no second chance to make a first impression.

Early in a project it is important to allow time for familiarisation. This will be necessary not only for practical matters (such as who's who, office layout, etc.) but also for understanding the informal rules and climate of the organisation. This I call a 'wallow'; it is unstructured data collection, which allows you to soak up the atmosphere and culture of an organisation, to learn its 'language', and so on.

Contracting

As soon as contact is made expectations will be created and commitments made on both sides. These are in addition to the formal agreement set out in the terms of reference (discussed in detail in Chapter 5).

- *Expectations* Relate not only to meeting commitments in the terms of reference, but also in how you carry out the project, eg the apparent priority you attach to the work you are doing for the client. You will also have expectations of the client; these will be reflected largely in the commitment the client shows towards the project.

- *Commitment* The sponsor – the member of the client's staff commissioning the project – will, presumably, be committed to it, but you have to consider the commitment of others. Will the project require the cooperation of more senior or more junior staff and, if so, are they committed to the project? Beware of sponsors who are not committed to the project or who are carrying it out as a personal crusade.

Organising

Organising covers the practicalities at the start of a project:

- Where will you be working, and with what facilities?

- What is the project plan? (If this has not been included in the terms of reference.)

- What support will you receive from the client, and what form will this take?

- Who will you be dealing with among client staff?

- What have client staff been told about the project (what are their expectations)?

Execution

Data collection and analysis

Paradoxically, you need to consider analysis before deciding what data you need to gather, you have to know what you are going to do with it when you have got it. Data gathering is time consuming, and you need to make sure you confine yourself to gathering only that which is necessary and sufficient for your purposes. (See Chapter 7.)

Diagnosis

The diagnosis should be drawn from the data collected and consists of conclusions about the nature of the problems being addressed and how they might be resolved. Conclusions answer the question, 'what is the relevance of this data to the areas of concern we are examining?'

Intervention

As a result of the diagnosis, you can then specify the intervention that needs to be made.

Because consultants rarely have executive authority within their clients, most often the intervention specified will be in the form of recommendations to be adopted by the client. Whether or not recommendations are accepted is, at least in part, dependent on the influence of the consultant; this topic is discussed at length in Chapter 8.

Withdrawal

The withdrawal stage has three aspects:

Transfer

When you leave the client, they should have an ongoing capability to maintain the changes and improvements you have introduced as a result of your work. Transfer is the process of so doing, and is discussed further in Chapter 8.

Evaluation

It is also important to carry out some sort of evaluation of the assignment once it has been completed. This is important not only for quality assurance purposes, but also to ensure that the consultancy practice gets value from the experience of the consultancy team who have carried out the job, for example by capturing:

- the experience of having carried out this work;

- any new operating techniques that have been developed during the project;

- the experience and credibility of working in a particular business sector.

Disengagement

The end of the project may mean the end of this particular piece of work, but there may be extension work – other projects you can carry out to the benefit of the client, or the continuation of the existing project to further levels. In any event, the experience of having worked together will have effected a change in the relationship between consultant and client, which should provide a good basis for further work in future.

2
PRODUCT DEVELOPMENT AND MARKETING IN CONSULTANCY

It was Ralph Waldo Emerson who wrote, 'If a man ... make a better mousetrap than his neighbour, tho' he build his house in the woods, the world will make a beaten path to his door.' However, your efforts will avail you naught if the world doesn't recognise the need for a mousetrap, or doesn't know you've built a better one, or has no idea where your door is.

This argument makes a case for marketing, but can you market consultancy? It has little tangibility, even by comparison with other services such as – say – dry cleaning, which have far more tangible outputs. Even so, consultancy is a product and, like other products, it needs to be marketed. Clearly, there are differences between consultancy and other product offerings. Figure 2.1 shows research that places consultancy in the context of other products, in a continuum in which consultancy and teaching (and much of consultancy has a training aspect) are shown at the 'intangible dominant' extreme.

Consultancy can be marketed, and because products and markets are so mutually dependent, I propose to treat marketing and product development together in this chapter. Selling consultancy is the subject of Chapters 3 and 4.

A simple distinction between marketing and selling consultancy services is that in selling you have a specific client in view; by contrast, marketing is to a specific sector – ie many prospective clients. Note that I have taken a limited definition of marketing as essentially the promotion of a consultancy firm and its services. Marketing purists would no doubt argue for a broader definition, emphasising the need for the business to be marketing oriented. Consultancy, however, is by

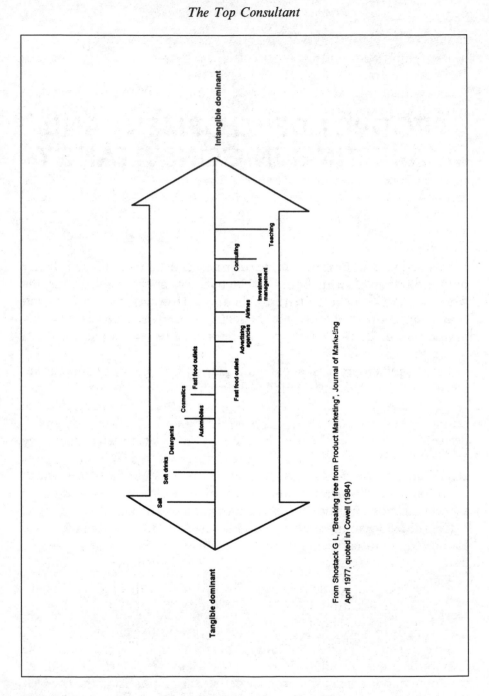

Figure 2.1 *A goods-service continuum*

nature a peculiarly market oriented business. Most people of any seniority in a firm – if not most consultants – have daily contact with their customers; few businesses outside the professions can boast as much contact. Moreover, every professional is called on to promote, if not sell, his or her firm's services, which again requires a strong market orientation.

It may seem surprising that there is product development in consultancy; some may view consultancy as simply providing the skills of consultants. What interests clients, however, is not just these skills, but how they may be applied to the advantage of the client's business. Product development consists of packaging the capabilities of a consultancy practice so that clients can more easily see the benefits of using the practice.

Marketing and product development in consultancy depend on the nature of the consultancy practice and the client, and the relationship between them. In this Chapter, therefore, we start with these topics, before moving on to the subjects of product development and marketing *per se*.

THE CONSULTANCY PRACTICE

Consultancy has evolved: over the last 20–30 years there have been three phases in management consultancy:

- *To the early/mid-70s* The consultant as the conduit through which the specialist knowledge of a practice was transmitted. Management consultancies' 'products' would consist of well-tried services or methodologies; the theory and practice of their introduction would be incorporated in manuals.

- *Early 70s–mid-80s* The consultant as 'management mercenary'. The consultant would be a generalist, perhaps with an MBA or some similar qualification. His or her role would be that of a gun for hire – a bright trouble-shooter who could take a new problem and resolve it from first principles. Previous experience was not essential; what was offered was a general skill.

- *Early 80s–present* The consultant as specialist. The consultant is hired because of the relevance of his or her skills to the problem in hand. Previous experience and personal expertise are important, but must be complemented with a capability to deliver specialist skills in a client environment.

Of course, these phases overlap. Plainly there were specialists operating before the mid-70s, and there are consultancy practices that offer proprietary approaches nowadays. In branches of consultancy outside management consultancy – IT consultancy, for example – the experience may also be different.

If there are signs of a trend for the 1990s, then it is that of the consultancy as a calculated source of added value to a business. The consultancy is there to enhance the competitive performance of the client. At the time of writing, in the UK, many consultancies have adopted a byline to this effect in all their advertising. Consultancies have to relate to the business as a whole.

The role of the consultant in the practice

A feature of the evolution described above is a trend from hiring a consultancy *per se* to hiring the *people* in the consultancy. Clients have become more discerning and are interested not only in the reputation of the practice, but also in the quality of the consultants put forward. It is therefore worth considering the provenance of people who become management consultants.

Many people become consultants having previously worked in specialist line positions. Indeed, management consultancies often draw their recruits from this source, and develop them by training and supervision in the skills required of a consultant.

Other specialists have chosen to become freelance consultants because they have been made redundant, or have taken early retirement. For many in this group, the notion of consultancy is not primarily about the professional skills involved, but more about their commercial relationship with those who are paying them – they are no longer employees, but self-employed contractors. Some will continue to confine their role to that of specialist subcontractor, while others will develop consultancy skills.

For those in a consultancy practice, there is a choice of role. Consultants can be simply the trained providers of a proprietary product, or promoted as experts in their own right. Each approach has its advantages and disadvantages. The practice with proprietary consultancy approaches will presumably market them as such, so a newcomer to the market has therefore not only to develop a new approach, and to prove that it is workable, but also to challenge the brand of the established provider.

By contrast, if the consultancy product is vested in the skills of an individual consultant, it is easy for the specialist to leave employment and take his or her skills – and possibly clients – to another employer, or set up alone as a sole practitioner. (This, of course, is how some of even the most venerable of the consultancies in the UK were started.)

Market segmentation and consultancy organisation

Many of the principles of traditional marketing apply to consultancy; they will not be repeated here. It is, however, worth mentioning the subject of segmentation. The need for consultancy services and the manner in which they are sold varies according to segment. The types of segmentation that consultancies use include:

- geographic;

- market sector;

- consultancy service or product.

This segmentation often provides the basis on which the consultancy practice is organised. Thus, a large consultancy may have a London office (geographic segmentation) in which there are specialists marketing IT consultancy services (consultancy service segmentation) to national government bodies (market sector). On the other hand, a sole practitioner may market his or her services in a specialist area of consultancy across the UK, irrespective of sector.

The comments in this chapter concern the consultancy practice as a whole, but can be applied to any specific segment.

THE NATURE OF THE CONSULTANCY CLIENT

The structure of business has changed radically since the early 1970s: whereas large corporations would then have had teams of in-house specialists to help with projects as and when required, the consequence of successive cost-cutting exercises has been that many specialist departments have closed. Specialist expertise is now resourced externally – not only in consultancy and other professions, but also in many other areas – office cleaning, running canteens, and so on. Activities that are not vital to the core of the business are subcontracted. (Charles Handy, in his book *The Age of Unreason*, sees this trend developing and greatly affecting the nature and structure of organisations.)

So consultancy has boomed. Whereas 20 years ago it would have been the norm for consultants to be employed because they had knowledge not possessed by the client, nowadays they might equally be taken on because the client does not have the volume of resources to tackle the problem.

Again, the growth of the consultancy business means that it is quite possible that a senior executive commissioning a consultancy project may have had a period of experience as a consultant (or will have worked with consultants before) and will be familiar with the techniques of selling and operating consultancy assignments. Clients have matured in their evaluation of the consultancy offering. This means that there is now a larger measure of equality between consultants and their clients. Moreover, as the use of consultants has become more widespread, so organisations have become more used to using consultants – there is less resistance to the idea of using them.

THE RELATIONSHIP BETWEEN THE PRACTICE AND THE CLIENT

At one extreme the relationship between the consultancy practice and the client is arm's-length; the consultancy is employed on a once-off basis to meet a specific need that the client is unable to meet from internal resources. At the other extreme there is an almost symbiotic relationship – the consultancy has been selected not only because of the value it can add to the client's business, but also because they feel comfortable doing business together – there is a good cultural match.

With the evolution of the consultancy business mentioned earlier, the typical relationship between consultancy practice and client has developed from the arm's-length sale to the alliance based on a long-term mutual benefit. Not all relationships between consultancies and their clients will be this close, of course; at the start, many will be on an arm's-length basis, anyway. The important point is that there has been a change in mind-set; a consultancy is not engaged in just a sale: it is developing an alliance. Long-term considerations apply, rather than just those relating to the immediate transaction with the client.

THE CONSULTANCY PRODUCT

Branding in consultancy

What are clients buying when they buy consultancy? Sometimes they may simply be seeking an independent view, or they may be augmenting their own resources because of the demands of a particular project. These cases simply define a consultancy as an external resource; but as we have noted above, consultancies are seeking to establish more durable relationships, with a greater exchange of value with their clients.

Consultancies therefore have a variety of offerings, which might be packaged as processes or methodologies. In so packaging its offerings, the consultancy will be building on experience, on analytical skills, or a mixture of both.

Having defined its offerings, the consultancy will need to decide how best to promote these in its target market sector(s). Here the notion of branding is helpful. Figure 2.2 shows how consultancy offerings relate to the type of branding.

At one end of the spectrum in Figure 2.2, the offering is shown as being about *services*. These are methodologies that are predefined, although their application may be tailored to the needs of a client. A

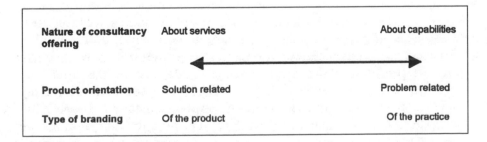

Figure 2.2 *The branding of consultancy offerings*

good example is a proprietary job-evaluation system, whose principles of operation and method of introduction to a business will be standardised, although the details will be varied according to each client's requirements. Such an offering is *solution-related* – ie the problem has already been defined. Under these circumstances, the *product* should be branded – eg the XYZ job-evaluation system.

At the other end of the spectrum, the offering is shown as being about *capabilities*. Practices in this position may offer an embracing methodology for working with clients in dealing with problems of a particular type. This is an approach to conducting assignments, rather than being related to a particular area of service. In these circumstances, Figure 2.2 suggests that the *practice* should be branded.

The difference between product and practice branding can be illustrated by an example from retail. Imagine that your aunt has been invited to a special event for which she needs a new outfit. She might say, 'I've no idea what to wear; I'll go along to Harrods to see if they have any ideas.' This is the equivalent of practice branding; she is going to Harrods because of the shop's reputation, but with no specific purchase in mind. Alternatively, however, she might say, 'I think I need a beige dress in classic style – I'll visit Oxford Street to see if I can find one.' This case is equivalent to product branding – she knows what she wants, and has to find someone to provide it.

In the context of consultancy, a firm may promote itself as 'specialists in managing change'. They have not said what kind of change they are involved in, and so are seeking to brand their practice. By contrast, another consultancy firm may offer a service called 'Office Move', dealing with all aspects of helping a business relocate. Businesses will be more attracted to 'Office Move' if they have decided that relocation is what is required.

There is some strategic advantage in branding the firm rather than the service. The prospective client may not be able to see the link between the service and the problem with which he or she is confronted (although the consultancy's promotional literature will seek to make this clear!). Unless the client can be persuaded to see the service as addressing the problem, then they may reject the consultancies offering these, preferring instead to go straight to those practices that specialise in the sort of problems confronting them. The providers of solutions are like a Chinese restaurant: if you want Chinese food, the ideal place to go, but not otherwise.

A further advantage for the firm branded as dealing with problems is that they will usually have to start with some diagnosis, ie a level 2 type intervention at least. (See Chapter 1 for the definition of levels of intervention.) This positions them well for follow-on work at levels 3 and 4, as well as extending the size of their market. By contrast, the client will have done much of the diagnosis for those offering solutions. For example, if approaching a recruitment consultant, a client will already have diagnosed the need for a recruit.

Given the advantages for the branded firm, consultancy firms will often have the strategic aim of moving from product branding to practice branding. The risk in doing this for those who are the providers of solutions only is that the results of their studies will always be the same – whatever the starting conditions, the same solution is prescribed. Like Henry Ford, they offer 'any colour, as long as it's black'.

Consultancy offerings must be communicable

Wherever it is positioned, the consultancy service has to be communicable. In the same way that a woodworker will find it difficult to describe his craft in terms other than the products he makes, so too consultants need to describe their services in terms of the processes used and the benefits arising from them.

In this respect, the firm with the branded service has an advantage. 'Recruitment' is far easier to discuss than 'capability in addressing issues around company culture'. Consequently new consultancies may wish to start by offering well-focused, clearly communicable services. Once these are established, the consultancy can start to abstract its offerings to capabilities, so as to become branded as a firm.

There are other similarities between the consultant and the woodworker. The job that the cabinet-maker does, for example, depends on the customer's specification. Similarly, the job done by the consultant consists of harnessing his or her skills to meet the requirements of the terms of reference as agreed. A difference, however, is that whereas the cabinet-maker can point to other items of furniture he may have created, it is less easy for the consultant to do so, because the product is intangible. This is commonly dealt with by using references from previous clients, or citing previous experiences, which can refer to the activities involved and the results achieved.

Another peculiarity of the consultancy offering is that to some extent it creates its own market. In this respect it is like innovative technology. The rapid growth in the use of fax machines in recent years shows how a piece of technology can create its own demand. Similarly, if consultants were to devise a method of reducing absenteeism among clients' employees, this could create its own market where none had previously existed.

PRODUCT DEVELOPMENT IN CONSULTANCY

To some extent, 'new' consultancy products offer old wine in new bottles. Skills in issue analysis, data collection, diagnosis and creating change, within a client environment, will be common to many consultancy offerings. In the same way that a cabinet-maker may change his designs to suit current fashion, management consultants focus their perennial skills on organisational matters of current concern – eg on cost reduction in a recession, on growth strategies in a boom.

Product development in consultancy is best described as the packaging of experience. The importance of a consultancy product being a communicable offering was explained above. It is more communicable if there is some sort of methodology that will lead to the results desired. Experience may be imported with a new recruit, or it may derive from experience in carrying out a consultancy assignment for a client – either way, if it is to be sold, it has to be packaged into a communicable offering. For example, some years ago a consultancy employed an expert in knowledge engineering for the first time – the only specialist of his kind within the firm. He had no previous experience of consultancy, and the consultancy was not quite clear what he had on offer. The results were that his specialist experience was never sold because it had not been packaged as a communicable offering.

Even when a consultancy has had some success in carrying out assignments in a particular area, there is some merit in 'packaging' this experience. If a consultancy had developed an approach that helped employers to reduce levels of absenteeism by half, this would be of great interest to large organisations. Few buyers, however, would have sufficient confidence to commission a consultancy project simply because the consultants asserted this was possible. Buyers would want to know how these results were achieved; they might want to talk to other clients for whom the consultants had done a similar job in the past. All these are steps that serve to reduce the sense of risk and increase confidence. Ultimately, all that a client gets when he or she buys a consultancy assignment is a promise. Packaging a consultancy product increases the client's confidence that the promise can be kept.

So what does a packaged consultancy product consist of?

- A name. At best, this can become a brand (eg 'the X job-evaluation system') or at the least make the reference to it simple (eg 'activity-based costing').

- An explanation of its purpose and the methodology used in carrying it out.

- Descriptions of situations in which it might be of use and the benefits of so doing.

- Information on previous applications of the technique and the benefits obtained.

Often a consultancy will publish a brochure describing the product; in this case, to the above list would be added information to meet the criteria set out in the section on marketing objectives, on p.43. Finally, if consultancy salespeople are to promote the product, they will find 'war stories' illustrating the benefits to be of great help, together with some indication of the likely costs of consultancy help.

There are some who, with some justification, claim that consultancy is a fashion business. The list of 'fashionable' products is extensive – portfolio analysis, quality circles, overhead value analysis, management by objectives, total quality management, were all popular in their time. And all have delivered value to their users, but may now be out of fashion. There is therefore a need on the part of consultancies – as with any other business – to maintain a flow of new products to meet the changing needs of their customers. Fashion may not be rational; but ignoring fashion in consultancy is like telling a couturier that the only purpose of clothing is to keep the rain off. And, to be fair, the delivery of 'old-fashioned' products can be improved with increasing experience, repackaged and relaunched.

Joint ventures and strategic alliances

In many respects, consultancy product development has similar characteristics to cookery. A skilled chef, working from a small range of ingredients, can create a wide variety of appealing dishes. In a similar way, consultants put together capabilities to create offerings attractive to clients.

Often certain capabilities are not available to a single firm of consultants and so they engage in joint ventures. 'Capabilities' in this context may not simply mean technical abilities – it might mean access to a market, or a depth of resource. For example, in entering a foreign market a consultancy might seek a joint venture partner.

Although it may not be involved in a strategic alliance, a large consultancy will be accustomed to forming consortia to bid for major projects. One prediction is that the major consultancies will slim down over the next few years, and concentrate on their core strengths. Increasingly they will draw the resources required for projects from subcontractors and joint ventures, working within a framework of the consultancy's own methodologies.

MARKETING CONSULTANCY

The aim of marketing is to:

- generate a demand for and raise awareness of a consultancy product;

- help to generate or identify good prospects;

- ease the extrinsic selling process (see Chapter 3 for a definition of this).

Marketing in a consultancy business therefore consists largely of promotional activities. There are, of course, professional restrictions on the methods by which consultants may promote themselves. The Institute of Management Consultants has laid down general guidelines for its members, which are set out in Appendix 1.

Some professions, such as chartered accountancy, do not allow the practice of 'cold calling' – making unsolicited contact with organisations with whom there has been no previous contact. The consultancy arms of such firms restricted thus (eg those associated with firms of accountants) are therefore similarly restricted. It is easy, however, to generate contacts; for example, some professional practices advertise a booklet or report which is available on application (eg by filling in a slip or coupon). Anyone who responds then finds themselves on the data base of contacts. The Institute of Management Consultants does not forbid cold calling, provided its guidelines are followed.

Who to market to

Research has shown that consultants get 80–90 per cent of their work from past clients and referrals; the remainder comes from sales promotion. Promotion is vital, however, as a flow of new clients is required to maintain a consultancy business, let alone grow it. This is because there is usually some client loss – a client may go out of business, or choose to use a competitor, or may even have no problems left that you can help with! So sales promotion is directed at prospective users of a consultancy's services.

Referrals – introductions and leads – come from *connectors*. Some professions are accustomed to using connectors – for example, accountants cultivate bankers to get introductions to the bankers' clients, and there can be a flow in the other direction. Connectors for consultants depend on the nature of the specialisation. Typically, referrals come from:

- existing or past clients;

- personal contacts;

- other consultancies (where not in competition);

- professional associations and brokers of consultancy expertise;

- other professional advisers.

In marketing to these, a consultancy aims to create a *network*. A strong network is necessary for all consultancies, whether sole practitioners or firms of more than a thousand professionals.

Often newcomers to consultancy underestimate the value of a good network. Junior consultants forget that they should cultivate their own networks as much as their more senior colleagues. In particular, they may be well positioned to identify and network with 'rising stars' in the client organisations with which they have worked.

Some two-thirds or more of a consultancy's business comes directly from past clients, and so they are obvious targets for receiving promotional material for new services. The advantages for a client in using the same consultancy for more than one assignment are that:

- they will have established an effective *modus operandi* for working together;

- the client will be confident in the consultant;

- the consultancy will have learned about the client and the client's business.

Sometimes these factors will outweigh other considerations; once (when working as a sole practitioner), a client said to me of a new piece of work he asked me to do, 'I realise that this is not at the centre of your expertise, but I think you can do a good job for us. You know us and we know you, which is far more important.' (Which is also very gratifying, provided you *can* do the job!) So existing clients should be a fruitful source of new business, in the form of additional services.

In large consultancies this presents a further need for marketing; no single individual can be in contact with all clients and know all the consultancy's services. There will be consultants who have account management responsibilities who themselves are specialists. They need to be informed of the other services the consultancy has on offer, and so a process of internal marketing has to be carried out in large practices. Account managers are internal connectors to the consultancy's clients, and so the provider of a specialist skill needs to promote it to these connectors as well as externally. Indeed, some commentators have estimated that in a large consultancy as much effort goes into internal marketing as external.

Promotional activities

Promotional activities can relate to the practice, the service, or the individual consultant.

Practices promote themselves through advertising and sponsorship. Some larger ones have even gone to the considerable expense of using TV advertising. The aim here is to promote general capability rather than a specific service. This is particularly appropriate for large practices with a wide range of services. Some make use of promotional films, which they can show to prospective new clients, again with the aim of promoting the strength of the practice. This is corporate advertising – something that large organisations in other sectors have practised for years.

The methods by which practices promote their services among prospective and existing clients include:

- brochures and other promotional publications;

- publishing house magazines or journals;

- articles in newspapers and magazines;

- carrying out, or sponsoring, research into a topic of interest, and making this available as a report;

- conferences, seminars, meetings, workshops, etc;

- entertainment – lunches, attendance at sporting occasions or other events.

The ways in which individuals in practices promote their services – or those of the practice – include:

- writing articles for newspapers and other periodicals or publishing books;

- appearances on TV or radio;

- membership of national or local bodies – professional associations, business or other societies.

The methods used to promote individuals and services can also be used to promote the practice as a whole. The Institute of Management Consultants offers helpful guidelines on promotion to its members, which are set out in Appendix 1.

Marketing objectives

There are five criteria that have to be satisfied before a client will issue an invitation to tender. They are:

1. The client has to recognise that a problem exists.
2. The client must believe that the problem is sufficiently important to merit attention.
3. The client must believe that the problem can be resolved.

4. The client must decide that outside help is required to resolve the problem.
5. The client must decide that your practice should be invited to tender for a project in this area.

The objectives of marketing should be to help to see that these criteria are satisfied. The consultancy which is attempting to market a new service may have to start at stage 1. At the other extreme, stages 1 to 4 may have been completed by the client without any prompting from a consultancy practice; it merely remains for the client to select a consultancy to work on the project.

Set out below are the activities you can undertake that will help to satisfy these criteria.

The client has to recognise that a problem exists

To go to a client offering a service to solve a problem which they do not recognise as such, stands as much chance of success as a plumber who wants to repair your central heating when nothing is wrong. Clients recognise problems in the following instances:

- When there is a problem or opportunity where previously none was thought to exist. Often these arise from change in the environment. For example:
  — concern with green issues;
  — repetitive strain injury;
  — employee counselling;
  — equal opportunities for women/minorities;
  — applications of chaos theory.
  All these changes represent features that have changed in the environment, which have led to consultancy opportunities. The job of the marketing consultant in these circumstances is to draw the attention of the client to the problem.

- When the problem is generally recognised, but the client did not know it occurred in his or her organisation. This is when data feedback is often used by consultants – for example a general survey of some feature of a business sector so that clients can compare the performance of their own organisation with those of others. Examples are the myriad personnel matters (pay, benefits, labour, turnover, etc) where there are hosts of surveys to which client organisations can subscribe.

The client has to believe that the problem is important

Organisations are rife with problems. Most of the problems are liveable with, or they eventually go away. No organisation can afford to be problem-free – there is a point of diminishing returns below which it is not worth tackling a problem. The way the consultancy markets in this respect is to show how the prospective returns are higher than the client originally thought.

Sometimes consultancies undertake a free survey to see whether a problem merits attention and, if so, what the likely return will be. For example, a consultancy that specialises in managing utility consumption (electricity, water, etc) might see whether any reduction in consumption can be achieved by using their own special techniques.

The client must believe that the problem can be resolved

There is the apocryphal story of the dictator who had two trays on his desk, one marked 'problems that time alone will solve', the other marked 'problems that time alone has solved'. It is hard to imagine such a non-interventionist dictator! In organisations, most people have plenty to do, so they do not want to waste their time attempting to resolve insoluble problems.

The task in marketing consultancy here is confidence building. If someone comes to you and says, 'I have a piece of kit which, attached to your car, will double your mileage per gallon of petrol,' you might be sceptical. However, if you were to be assured by other users whose opinions you trusted that this was the case, then you might buy the kit. A reputation for success helps enormously.

The client must want outside help

Much though it might go against the consultant's grain, organisations can solve their problems for themselves. Sometimes the competition for a consultant lies with the client's own staff rather than another consultancy. The table below sets out some benefits of each.

Of course these are not exclusive benefits. A consultancy may know a long-established client very well; alternatively, an internal member of

Table 2.1 *Relative benefits of using outside consultants and internal staff*

Benefits of outside consultants	Benefits of internal staff
Objective	Know the organisation well
Is an additional resource	Have to be paid anyway
Experienced at dealing with this type of project	Experienced at dealing with the organisation
Can change consultant personnel if client not satisfied	High incentive to please this client (employer!)

staff may be very expert at dealing with the type of problem to be resolved.

The job of consultants in marketing themselves at this point is to show how well-equipped they are to address this type of problem, which is the purpose of promotional material.

The client must want your help

The last stage – deciding that your consultancy firm should be invited to tender for a particular project – is the essential component of selling, which is dealt with in Chapters 3 and 4.

3
SALES STRATEGY IN CONSULTANCY

If you are sick and want treatment, you must go to a doctor. If you run a company, you are required to have an auditor. If you have legal problems, you need to consult a lawyer. Nobody *has* to have a management consultant. Consultants must therefore sell their services actively if they are to survive.

Simple arithmetic shows the commercial imperative to sell in a consultancy practice. Assume you have a medium-sized firm with 25 consultants who are paid, on average, £40,000 pa. Assume that fully absorbed on-costs and overheads are as much again as their salaries. The annual expenses of that consultancy will be £2m. The fee income has to be £8,000 per working day just to cover costs. Sales of consultancy work obviously have to equal this if the firm is to break even.

It is a fortunate business that can generate sales at this level without any selling effort. Selling has to be active. If professionals are to be able to pursue their calling, there has to be an economic base sufficient to support them. The same applies to internal consultants. Although they may be 'free of charge', they receive a salary and incur other costs; they too have to justify their existence commercially.

Selling is thus vital to any consultancy practice. But the purpose of this chapter is not to iterate the general principles of selling – there are plenty of excellent books on these. Nor is it going to cover the traditional selling of services – I have always found it difficult to learn much from likening consultancy to a restaurant, supermarket or plumbing service. Consultancy has some peculiar features even in comparison with other professional services, such as law and accountancy; for example, it has more often to provide a service unique to the client and occasion.

It is said that the skilled salesperson can sell anything, which implies that there is a set of selling skills that are universally applicable. Whether this is true is debatable. Certainly there will be salespeople who find little difficulty in making the transition to selling consultancy from selling more tangible items. But there are several significant differences between these activities, and understanding the implications of these differences will help in selling consultancy. Likewise, the consultant who has no previous selling experience needs some guidance as to the appropriate sales processes to use in selling consultancy.

In this chapter, therefore, we examine those processes, while in Chapter 4 we will deal with the practical aspects of selling. But first we consider the challenges for the two types of person mentioned above each of whom is now called on to sell consultancy:

- the salesperson who has had previous experience in selling but little or none in consultancy;

- the technical specialist who has experience in consultancy, but little or none in selling.

CHALLENGES FOR THE EXPERIENCED SALESPERSON

Even products that can be customised are usually broadly predefined offerings, which may be tailored in detail to the needs of the client. Much of the time, consultancy is the opposite. It starts with identifying the needs of the client (or responding to a set of needs as embodied in an invitation to tender) and then putting together an offering that helps the client to address these needs.

This means that – unless you are a consultant with a single product only – it is unusual to sell consultancy by going to a client with a preconception of what you are going to sell him. Selling is more often about spotting opportunities than creating needs. The implications for you if you are a traditional salesperson are therefore:

- Each consultancy project is a uniquely tailored offering. A car salesman might sell from a product catalogue; the only variations are the extras that a customer might want. In consultancy, the sales process also involves product specification.

- You must listen to clients' requirements and respond with offerings that reflect their needs.

- If you work for a large firm of consultants, you cannot have a comprehensive knowledge across all fields of its consultancy offerings, and so you will need to involve specialists in support selling.

The role of salesperson in consultancy is more one of facilitator than 'hero'. You have to create opportunities that others will help to realise.

Figure 3.1 shows the critical dimensions in thinking about the role of the salesperson. The figure shows two extremes; it is unlikely that any sales activity will be wholly at one end or the other, but will be somewhere in between. What the figure points out, though, is the *thrust* in selling consultancy – for most salespeople, the challenge lies in moving towards the right in the diagram.

The spectrum of selling is shown from being transaction-oriented to relationship-oriented. A salesperson who is strongly transaction-oriented will be impelled to close the sale. In an extreme form this is typical of the high-pressure salesperson, who has a prime objective to ensure that you buy.

Most salespeople who want repeat business recognise early in their careers that they cannot be wholly transaction-oriented. Of course, the quotas and targets that they are set are usually related to sales volume – no points for having wonderful relationships and no sales – but they will be anxious to preserve a good relationship with their customers.

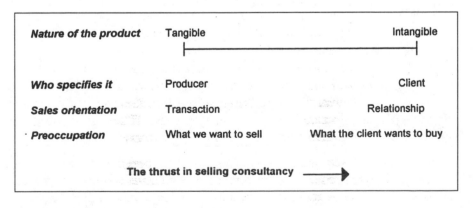

Figure 3.1 *The selling spectrum*

Consultancy, too, has quotas and targets, but the need for a good relationship is even greater than with other products. When buying a tangible item you can see an example of what you will get; in consultancy you buy only a promise. Even if the consultancy has a proven track record, this is no guarantee of success on this occasion; it simply reduces the sense of risk. So there has to be a high level of trust between the salesperson and his or her client. But as with other successful client relationships, once they are firmly established, consultancy clients become a fruitful source of continuing business.

CHALLENGES FOR THE TECHNICAL SPECIALIST

There are challenges for the technical specialist who becomes involved in selling. As for the salesperson, there will be some who take to it very easily; others find it difficult to accept a sales role. Some specialists feel selling is 'unprofessional', and are most uncomfortable when called on to do it.

In such circumstances they may rely on their technical expertise, or the warmth of their relationships with the client to secure the sale. But as Figure 3.2 shows, there are three factors that combine to influence the sales performance of a professional:

1. Technical skills – the specialist skills of the consultant.
2. Interpersonal skills – in the short term, these are the skills of

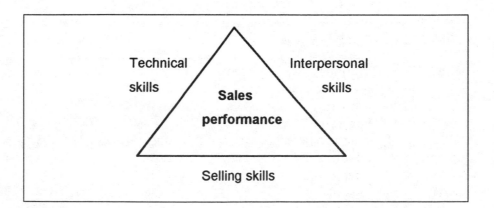

Figure 3.2 *Factors influencing sales performance*

conducting effective personal relationships: in the longer term, they are manifest as the consultant's network, which needs to be established, maintained and developed.
3. Selling skills – understanding buying and selling processes in consultancy, and capability in identifying opportunities and developing sales.

All three are important. The area of the triangle in Figure 3.2 depends on the length of all three sides – if the length of one side is nil, then the area will be nil. If the area of the triangle represents sales performance, all three skills must be represented to achieve a satisfactory standard of sales performance. What consultants – and other professionals – often feel reluctant to admit is that selling skills are important. The diagram shows, however, that selling skills are just as important as the other two areas of skill.

Technical skills create reputation

Ultimately, the capacity to execute assignments well will be the measure of a consultancy practice's success. Reputation counts for a lot; in my first week as a consultant I was told, 'One bad job costs 100 good ones'. Satisfied clients act as connectors; and satisfied individuals who change jobs introduce their favoured consultants to their new employers. Technical skill creates a favourable reputation, which helps the extrinsic sales process (see below).

Interpersonal skills create a network

As noted before, all experienced salespeople recognise the need for their activities to be relationship-led rather than transaction-led if they are to achieve more than a single sale. Common sense suggests that we will buy more from the salesperson we like than one to whom we are indifferent, other factors being equal.

Because of the nature of the consultancy product, far more emphasis has to be placed on the relationship. The reason is that – despite references and reputation – when a client buys a consultancy assignment, it is on trust. The project may be expensive and of considerable importance; a buyer may have staked his or her reputation on its success. Before doing this, he or she must have the confidence that it will be successful. It is unlikely that this will be the case unless there is a good relationship with the consultant. This relationship has to be underwritten by good work, however. If the consultant (or consultancy) has previously carried out high-quality work, the client will be more inclined to give them more. This is supported by evidence that some two-thirds of consultancy work derives from existing or previous clients.

During your work, you will build up a network of relationships with people who are employed by past or prospective clients, professional contacts, and so on. 'Networking' is about maintaining these relationships. Even if the activity is not directly related to a sale, there are benefits in networking:

- getting market intelligence;

- obtaining leads and introductions;

- raising awareness of your firm and its services;

- maintaining the network.

Time spent on networking has to be invested with a purpose; it is easy to be a busy fool, and there are time-wasters, as there are in any other area of activity. The evidence is, however, that 80–90 per cent of a consultancy's sales come from its network, some two-thirds from repeat business and the remainder from referrals. So consultants have to be active in creating and maintaining their networks.

Creating and maintaining networks can be done quite easily – by attending business or professional meetings, or even over lunch. I remember sitting at lunch with a partner in a firm of consultants (with whom I was networking!) who complained about his consultant team, 'As we sit here, they are all sat at their desks eating sandwiches. Why aren't they out networking?'

Selling skills are needed to create sales

Shortly after I started my first job as a management consultant there was one of those periodic downturns in the market. All consultants are exhorted to sell, and in a recession we were doubly so. Being young and enthusiastic, I started to try to sell to my (limited) network. I had a simple technique: 'Consultancy is jolly good, and so is my firm. Why don't you buy an assignment?'

I was totally unsuccessful, because I had no selling skills. The unhappy truth is that technical skills and a good relationship will create few sales by themselves. Some selling skills are also required.

Given that a consultant's stock in trade is time, a critical measure of performance in managing a consultancy practice is the amount of time it takes to win a sale. A simple example illustrates this. Imagine that a one-man consultancy practice has 180 days available for work each year, after allocating time to holidays, training and administration. The consultant has set a revenue target of £75,000 for the year. If his sales ratio is 50 per cent, this means that he has to spend one day selling to generate two days' work. (This selling time would include pursuing unsuccessful prospects, as well as successful sales.) This means that he has to spend 60 days selling to generate 120 days' work. To reach his revenue target, his fee rate has to be (£75,000/120 =) £625 per day. If, however, he was a more successful salesman with a sales ratio of 20 per cent, he would generate five days of sales for each day spent selling. In his year of 180 days, therefore, he would spend 30 days selling and 150 days operating. He would therefore need to charge only £500 per day to reach his target revenue. Alternatively, were he to charge the same as he would need to if he were less effective (ie £625 per day), his annual income would be increased by £18,750 – 25 per cent.

The reason, therefore, for being concerned with selling performance is to optimise this sales ratio. There are two important skills that contribute to successful selling performance:

- *Qualification*   Choosing which prospective clients to pursue. This is important, because it relates to the effective use of time. The consultancy salesperson should be devoting his or her time to pursuing those prospects that are most likely to produce sales.

- *Conversion*   Moving a prospect along to the next stage of the sales process.

We therefore need to have a model of the selling process; a simplified model is shown in Figure 3.3 below.

Marketing activities should enable you to identify prospective clients, or result in enquiries from them. Not every sales opportunity will necessarily be pursued; this is part of the qualification process.

Having identified suitable prospects, the next goal is to be invited to tender a proposal for carrying out some consultancy work through the

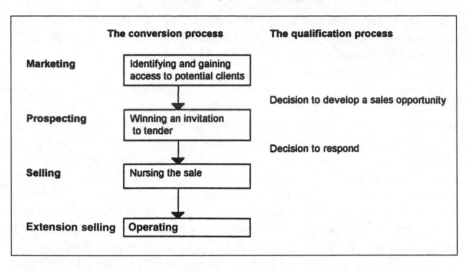

Figure 3.3 *Simplified model of the selling process*

activity of *prospecting*. A consultancy may not wish to respond to every invitation to tender, so qualification is again applied here.

Once a proposal is submitted, there may be further selling activity to get it accepted by the client. When the sale is made, operating work can start on the consultancy project, and the consultancy team will look for other areas where the consultancy practice can work with the client; this is the extension selling process.

In this chapter we shall unravel this process further, looking at the different strategies that might be followed in selling. In Chapter 4, the practical skills required in face-to-face client transactions will be considered. First, however, it is important to recognise that there are two different aspects involved in the selling process.

EXTRINSIC AND INTRINSIC SELLING

Imagine that you have just moved house; you have a solicitor who has carried out the conveyancing for you. At your final meeting with her, you remark that you will need to install a new central heating system in your house. Your solicitor then says, 'Oh, I can do that for you – I practise plumbing as well as law.'

Now, it may well be that your solicitor is the best and cheapest plumber to do this job, but you would need some convincing to accept her in this role. If she was to persuade you to consider her services, she would have to engage in *extrinsic selling*.

Extrinsic selling legitimises the seller as a provider of a product or service. In the example above, the solicitor would have to convince you that she is indeed a bona fide plumber before you even started to discuss the work that you need doing.

So extrinsic selling is persuading the prospective client that the consultancy practice is worth doing business with in the first place. By contrast, *intrinsic selling* is persuading the client of the merit of a particular proposition. Intrinsic selling will not be successful unless the extrinsic sales process has been completed, and completing the extrinsic sales process does not imply success in completing the intrinsic one. Continuing the example above, even if your solicitor does convince you that she can install your new heating system, you might seek quotations from other plumbers to make sure that her quotation is competitive and, if it isn't, you would choose another. Likewise, you will not work – say – with an insurance broker unless you are convinced that he will probably give you the service you want (the extrinsic process). On the other hand, you will not necessarily accept every suggestion he makes concerning the insurance policies you might invest in (the intrinsic process).

Every sale consists of these two stages of extrinsic selling followed by intrinsic selling. Given the importance that has already been cited of managing time effectively in selling, then the less time that has to be spent on extrinsic selling, the more that can be spent on the intrinsic stage – making specific sales.

Marketing and promotion help the extrinsic sales process for a consultancy. Chapter 2 on marketing consultancy described branding products or practices within consultancy. The value of a brand is that it helps with extrinsic selling. If your consultancy practice is well-known for its skill in introducing production control systems, then less effort is required to legitimise your consultancy offering in this area to a specific client. On the other hand, the same consultancy would have greater difficulty in selling assignments in – say – marketing, unless it was equally well-known in its target market for this.

Less effort is required in selling extrinsically to existing clients – they have already accepted your bona fides as a consultant. It is for this reason that consultants sell mainly to their existing client base. From the client's point of view, too, there are advantages in dealing with the same consultant. It takes time to educate a consultant into the ways of a client's business. Dealing with a consultant used in the past avoids this time and cost.

It is worth noting that some extrinsic selling is required when seeking to sell new products or services to existing clients. This is vividly exemplified by IT hardware suppliers in the early 1990s. Faced with increasing competition and diminishing margins in their traditional markets, they enlarged their services to include IT and management consultancy. This presented a challenge to their sales forces. Say the names of any hardware supplier to a client and they would think of them as a hardware supplier; there was no need to legitimise them as such. When it came to their services as consultants, however, salespeople had for the first time to engage much more in extrinsic selling.

THE SALES PROCESSES

The sales processes involved in finding new clients, or generating more sales from an existing customer base, are known as *hunting* and *farming* respectively.

Traditionally, a hunter goes out to find his quarry – departing from his home territory to wherever his quarry might be found. In like manner, the hunter-salesperson goes out beyond the existing client base to find new clients. By contrast, the farmer stays on his home land and uses that to produce the food required; the farmer-salesperson produces new sales from an existing client base.

In consultancy the process of hunting is often called *prospecting* (as in prospecting for gold), and farming is called *extension selling* – ie selling an extension to a current assignment. Both hunting and farming are necessary, but salespeople often have a preference and aptitude for one rather than the other.

The strategic model of hunting

Figure 3.4 shows the strategic model of hunting as a sort of target; the closer to the bull's eye, the better the chances of success.

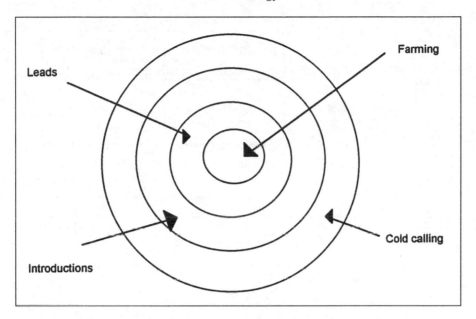

Figure 3.4 *Hunting: Selling to new clients – strategic model*

At the centre is shown farming; the link between hunting and farming is described in the strategic model of farming. Moving out from the bull's eye are shown *leads* and *introductions*. Both are kinds of referral via a connector. An introduction is to a client who might need your consultancy services. A lead is more than an introduction, in that the connector has seen an immediate requirement for the type of consultancy you might offer.

Cold calling is the least fruitful of hunting activities as, in the words of one salesperson, 'You have to kiss a lot of frogs before you find a prince'. Cold calling with a telephone call out of the blue is least likely to work; 'warming up' clients is important so that they will be more receptive to that telephone call when it does come.

The strategic model of farming

There are different ways in which sales can be made to an existing client base; as mentioned above, sometimes it can be closer to hunting. Figure 3.5 shows the strategic model of farming.

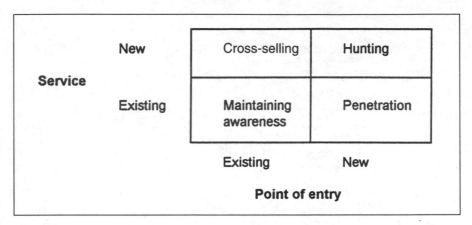

Figure 3.5 *Farming: Selling to existing clients – strategic model*

A small organisation may have only one purchaser of consultancy, but large ones have many. You may therefore seek new points of entry to existing clients. Similarly, you may try to sell services other than those being purchased already.

You need first to ensure that existing clients continue to use your practice to supply services as in the past. For example, a consultant in logistics would want to secure all consultancy work in this area from an existing client. If the client gave an assignment to a competitor, this would place the consultant's business under threat. So you have to nurture existing clients so that your firm is the one that comes to mind when new opportunities arise for your services. This is about *maintaining awareness*.

Selling new services to an existing point of entry is called *cross-selling*; establishing new points of entry with an existing client is *penetration*. If the salesperson is seeking to sell new services to a new point of entry, this is an activity similar to hunting, when you can get warm leads and introductions from one part of the organisation to another.

The hunting sales process

Figure 3.6 shows the sales process for hunting.

The process starts with *suspects* – those organisations that might need your consultancy services. If yours is a large consultancy, then all

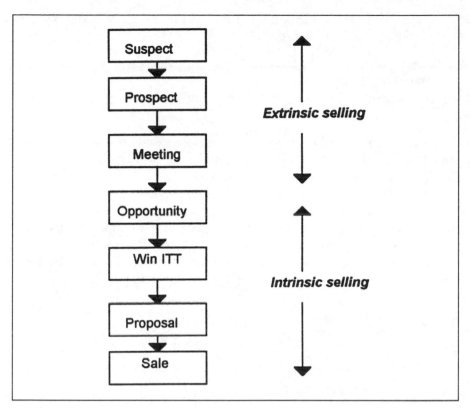

Figure 3.6 *Hunting: Selling process*

organisations might be suspects for the full range of your services. (Size is not necessarily a limit; I have worked for one of the largest corporations in the world in the same year that I also worked for an organisation of only six people.) Such a large number of suspects is not helpful, and so it is best to look at them according to consultancy product. The suspects might also be limited by market segmentation (eg geography or industrial sector).

From this long list of suspects you would select a shorter list of companies to approach – ie *prospects*. These might be selected against criteria such as:

- *A need for your service* This might be general (eg organisations are usually interested in worthwhile ideas for increasing performance) or event-driven (eg a company that has just made a new acquisition, or expanded into a new market).

- *Ease of access* For example, you might choose to avoid companies that you know have a good relationship with one of your competitors who can supply the same consultancy services that you are trying to sell.

The next stage is to warm up the prospect so that they will agree to a *meeting*. This is a limited objective – ie the approach is not to get the prospect to buy, but to secure the meeting – or to disqualify the organisation as a prospect (see below under 'Qualification').

The purpose of the meeting is to get an invitation to tender a *proposal* (ITT) for consultancy services. If the client accepts this, perhaps after some negotiation, the sale is made.

Note that in this sales process, there has to be considerable extrinsic selling activity before you can engage in intrinsic selling. This is in

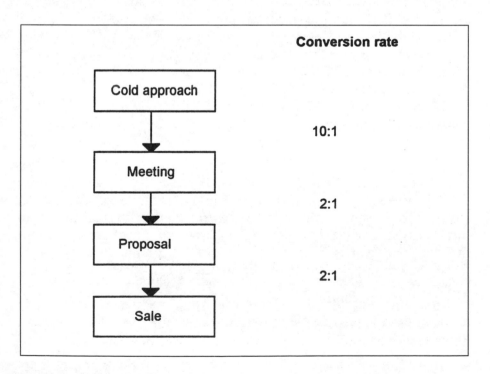

Figure 3.7 *The sales process*

marked contrast to the farming selling process (see below). The whole process can be thought of as a leaky pipeline; at each stage, prospective clients will drop out until only a few are left that lead to sales. Figure 3.7 shows the ratios that were calculated by one consultancy salesman.

Clearly the ratios will vary with time, product, market and salespeople. On the figures shown, on average of the 40 prospects he started with, only one resulted in a sale. The significance of this is that if you are to be a successful hunter:

- You have to start with a large number of organisations that you believe could be clients for your service.

- You have to accept a lot of 'noes' with only a few 'yeses'.

The farming sales process

Figure 3.8 shows the sales process for farming. By contrast with hunting, it involves mainly intrinsic selling; the consultancy practice is already legitimised as a provider of consultancy services.

The 'end-game' – winning the invitation to tender, submitting the proposal and converting it to a sale – is similar to that for hunting. Where it differs is that the early stages are associated with identifying opportunities within a specified client.

The easiest form of selling is where a client contacts you with a consultancy opportunity and asks for help. Contrast this with the hard work required to get to this point in hunting, where sales performance will be much lower. Clients will initiate contact only if they have some idea of the services and capabilities you have on offer, so raising and maintaining your clients' awareness of them is important. This is the task of promotional marketing, which was dealt with in Chapter 2.

The other method of farming shown in Figure 3.8 is for the consultancy to be proactive, taking the initiative to develop further sales with existing clients. Strictly speaking, it should not be optional – a consultancy should be proactive anyway. Opportunities can be developed by the consultancy when:

- there is an event of some significance for the client (eg an announcement of business expansion, the loss of a key customer);

- there is a major change in the client's market sector (eg new regulatory or environmental restrictions);

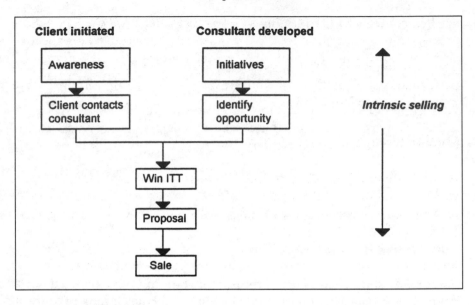

Figure 3.8 *Farming: Selling process*

- you have a new service that could be of interest to the client;

- there is significant development among the client's competitors, which could result in a loss of competitive position;

- you have a strong view about an operational or strategic aspect of the client's business, and want to draw the client's attention to this.

On this last point it is worth emphasising that I do believe that consultants can be advocates. It is in our interests to have successful clients – a consultancy firm will not flourish if its clients go out of business. If, therefore, as a consultant you can see an opportunity for a client to develop their business performance, then you should make representations about it. Indeed, the account management process in some practices has been formalised in respect of creating opportunities, rather than leaving it to chance. Someone in the consultancy account team will have the responsibility for looking ahead at the future needs of the client and making plans for how these are to be met, where appropriate, by providing consultancy support.

DEVELOPING SALES PERFORMANCE

The two important skills mentioned above that contribute to sales performance are qualification and conversion. If sales performance is to improve, each of these must get better.

Qualification

At each stage of the sales process there is a need for qualification – which clients should be converted to the next stage of the sales process, or which sales opportunities with a particular client should be pursued.

Obviously clients may disqualify themselves (as is shown by the conversion experience shown in Figure 3.7); a sales call may be unsuccessful, or a prospect may not agree to a meeting. What is particularly hard for the salesperson, however, is to disqualify a client from the consultancy's point of view. It is hard because the salesperson may well have put much effort in to nursing the prospect to this stage in the sales process.

There are several obvious reasons for disqualification. Some people love to chat to consultants and to pick their brains, with no assignment ever in view. If the assignment in view is one that the consultancy cannot do, or is of questionable ethics, or involves an actual conflict of interest, then the opportunity may also be disqualified.

Early in the prospecting process, therefore, you should assess the probability of a consultancy project deriving from your efforts. To this end, you should check that:

- there is a genuine need for consultancy work of the kind that the consultancy can offer;

- the prospective client intends to offer this to outside consultants;

- the individuals with whom you are dealing have the budget and authority to proceed with the project, or can act as connectors to such individuals.

Qualification is particularly crucial at the time of submitting a proposal, not only because the task of preparing a proposal is time consuming, but also because the proposal is a commitment by the consultancy to carry out a specified assignment.

Before offering to submit a proposal, therefore, you should consider the following points:

- Is the consultancy able to carry out the work, in terms of the competence and availability of resources?

- What are the risks involved, and are they acceptable? Risks assessed include:
  — the financial standing of the client;
  — political risks;
  — the difficulty of achieving the project deliverables;
  — the complexity and size of the project.

- Will undertaking the project produce any conflicts of interest with other clients?

- Will undertaking the project produce any conflicts of interest with other parts of the consultancy?

- Is there a serious chance of winning the assignment?

Salespeople are strongly impelled to make sales and so there is the temptation to bid in response to every invitation to tender. The failure to qualify properly, however, can result either in wasting time, or committing to projects that are unprofitable at best.

Conversion

The other important skill in achieving a high standard of sales performance is that of conversion – the ability to develop clients along the sales process. This is a transactional skill – a skill in communicating with the client face-to-face, by telephone, letter, and so on. This is an extensive subject and so merits a chapter of its own – see Chapter 4.

Suffice to note at this point that it is sensible to monitor your success at conversion at each stage of the sales process, and to research the reasons for success or failure. By monitoring conversion performance you can identify areas of strength and weakness, and develop a better idea of what practices will help you to optimise your conversion rate.

4
PRACTICAL SELLING IN CONSULTANCY

It is always fascinating to get feedback from clients on their perceptions of consultants. I belong to a group of freelance consultants who, from time to time, organise a clients' forum at which selected clients are invited to give feedback on their experience in using consultants. At one of these forums a client, who had invited tenders for a consultancy contract worth £500,000, commented on the mixture of responses he got.

> The worst compensated for their incompetence by their arrogance; they couldn't answer simple questions. The ones we appointed were the opposite – technically excellent. Moreover they were sensitive to the cost implications of the project and ensured we had the financial resources to implement the changes required.

Another client commented, 'The consultant made it easy for us to buy – it was not hard work for us. At no time did we feel that we were being sold to.'

One of my associates talks about organisations that seem to have a 'sales prevention department'. Presumably no organisation has the aim of preventing sales, any more than a salesperson would wish to have the negative effect quoted above. Yet everybody who is involved in selling will have experienced occasions when they leave a sales meeting knowing that they have failed. The failure is not that the customer did not want to buy – that possibility has always to exist if you want to be anything more than a high-pressure salesperson. The failure is because the customer might well have bought, but poor selling technique resulted in the failure to convert the opportunity to a sale.

There are no techniques that will guarantee success in selling consultancy every time. There are techniques, however, which will increase the probability of success by improving your selling performance. In this chapter, therefore, we start by outlining the objectives, process and basic skills involved in selling. Each step in the selling process is then described.

PRINCIPLES OF EFFECTIVE SELLING

Selling objectives

Consultancy may appear to a client to be an undifferentiated product; if the client has specified what is to be achieved and the steps towards this, then any capable consultant could probably deliver. Differentiation must therefore lie not only in the consultancy service, but also in the quality of its delivery.

Differentiation of delivery starts in the sales process, so what should you be seeking to achieve in this? Wittreich, in a seminal article (Wittreich, 1966) suggested there are three objectives in selling professional services:

1. *Minimizing uncertainty* – A professional service must make a direct contribution to the *reduction of the uncertainties* involved in managing a business. The proper assessment of a service, unlike tangible goods, usually must take into account the impact of its performance on the client's business.
2. *Understanding problems* – A professional service must come directly to grips with a fundamental problem of the business purchasing that service. The successful performance of the service, far more so than the successful production of a product, depends on an understanding of the client's business.
3. *Buying the professional* – A professional service can only be purchased meaningfully from someone *who is capable of rendering the service*. Selling ability and personality by themselves are meaningless.

The importance of these concepts has been endorsed by research in the UK. In 1988, KPMG Peat Marwick McLintock published the findings of some research they had commissioned from MORI. Figure 4.1 shows the relative levels of importance of factors involved in selecting a management consultancy which the survey indicated.

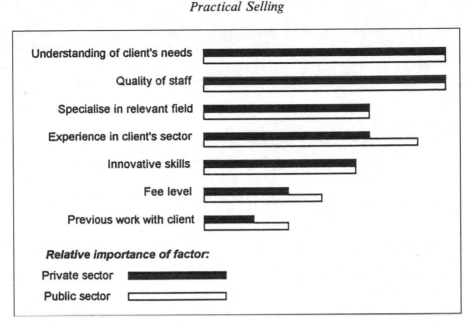

Figure 4.1 *Selecting a management consultancy*

One of the two factors ranked as most important is 'having a real understanding of your needs' – confirming Wittreich's statements number 1 and 2 above.

Many of the other factors relate to the quality of the people – Wittreich's third point. In a large consultancy practice, however, the person who is the account manager – maybe a partner or director of the practice – will not necessarily be delivering the service. This is when team selling is used, and this is covered later in this chapter.

Although fee levels are shown to be comparatively less important, they can be instrumental in the buying decision in competition when:

- other features of competing firms are very similar;

- there is a significant difference in the amounts quoted.

The fact that 'previous experience with your firm' comes so low in the order of priorities seems to contradict the comments made in Chapters 2 and 3 about existing clients being the most fertile ground. The same survey, however, notes the finding that business colleagues were the most important source of information about management consultancies. Previous work together may not be significant in the intrinsic selling process (ie securing a particular assignment), but is important in getting you through the door in the first place (ie being invited to tender).

The selling process

There are three steps involved in practical selling:

1. Getting access to a prospect; this is dealt with in this chapter under the heading of 'Winning a meeting'.
2. Conducting sales meetings, which should lead to an invitation to tender (ITT). (An ITT need not be a formal document – it can be an oral request from a prospect for you to put in a proposal.)
3. Converting the ITT to a sale – dealt with under the heading of 'Winning the sale'.

The framework within which this approach is applied may be *ad hoc*, or it might be part of a focused, proactive sales campaign to get new clients.

Large consultancies, with extensive networks, may have no difficulty getting access to a specific target. With greater resources than small practices, they may invest more in selling to a specific target prospect. For example, they may prepare a detailed presentation, free of charge, on an aspect of the client's business where the consultancy believes there to be a good opportunity of working together. Even with good contacts, however, the number of times you can 'cash in' on a relationship is limited. You can exercise a key contact – say – a couple of times a year, but goodwill on their side will disappear if they feel the meetings are of little value.

Selling skills are needed in all cases. In what follows I have assumed that you cannot command the attention of the target, and so have to follow a more general sales process. The three steps listed above map on to the general model of the sales process presented in Figure 3.3, as shown in Figure 4.2 below.

Before explaining these steps, however, we will review some of the basic skills required in the selling process.

Basic skills in selling

The danger of being dogmatic over any aspect of selling is that there is

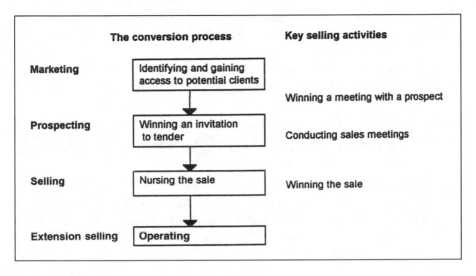

Figure 4.2 *Key activities in the selling process*

almost certainly a salesperson somewhere who, despite breaking any rule you care to mention, is being enormously successful. In many ways, the choice of method of approach is a personal one. Just as the same style of dress would not suit everybody, so too do different salespeople have different styles.

The initial contact with a prospect is crucial, in that it forms the background to the sales activity that follows. Making the initial contact is perhaps one of the most stressful parts of the sales activity for the salesperson. The following tips, therefore, although generally applicable in selling consultancy, should be particularly helpful when approaching a prospect for the first time.

- Listen. In consultancy the emphasis is on the prospect specifying what they want and why they want it. You can respond only if you listen to what they have to say.

- Have a positive vision of your transactions with your prospects. If you expect a successful outcome, you are more likely to achieve it than if you expect to fail. Failure is the likely outcome if you are about to make a phone call to a prospect and have an internal video running that says 'They won't put me through. Even if they do, I'll say all the wrong things. Mr Prospect will ask me all sorts of questions I won't know the answer to ...' etc, etc. Contrast this with a view that says 'I expect to be put through. This will give me the opportunity to have a mutually beneficial discussion with Mr Prospect', etc.

You should, therefore, aim to begin with a positive rather than negative expectation of the encounter. Write out the positive scenario on a card. Before making a telephone call or entering a meeting, read it to yourself. Gradually the positive attitude should begin to take over.

- In particular, you should have a positive vision of your relationship with the prospect. If you see yourself as a supplicant seeking the boon of his or her custom, this will show, and the prospect will treat you as an inferior. The picture you should have in your mind is that of fellow professionals with a shared interest in the improvement of the prospect's business. Of course, you will wish to maintain a professional relationship with your clients on matters to do with work, but this does not imply superiority or inferiority; the client is an expert in his or her area of work, as you are in yours.

There are clients who want their ego massaged (don't we all to some extent!). If you don't like doing this then, in cases where it is necessary, you must relinquish the client to someone who is good at ego massage!

WINNING A MEETING

In winning the meeting, there are three steps:

1. Identify the prospect organisation to which you wish to sell.
2. Find out which person you should contact.
3. Approach the prospect with the aim of winning a meeting at which you can present your services.

Identifying prospects

If clients are not forming a queue at your door to do business with you (and if they are, why not put up your fees?) then you have to find new clients. Let us assume that you have to find these by hunting. Some criteria for identifying prospects are suggested in Chapter 3; in any case, you should draw up a prospect profile, ie the key characteristics of an organisation likely to buy your services.

You then have to identify the organisations and individuals within them where you have a good chance of being able to sell your services. You might start by referring to a business directory. Often, however, a directory will give insufficient information about a business for you to qualify them adequately, so some further research needs to be done to find out more. Annual reports and advertising material will provide additional useful data. Other sources include newspaper cuttings and other information services that can be accessed via business libraries and some of which are computer-based.

This will enable you to eliminate those suspects who are not good prospects. The next stage is to approach the prospect.

Who to sell to

Whereas organisations may have sophisticated systems for specifying and purchasing hardware, these are rarely matched by the processes for buying consultancy. In selling assignments, you may find yourself in the position of having to guide the prospect through the buying process. The consultancy sales process is directed towards this, involving, as it does, clarifying exactly what the prospect wants (see Chapter 5 for more on this).

The old adage in selling is 'sell to the MAN' – the person who has the money, authority and need. (More recently, the acronym WOMAN has also been used, to avoid charges of sexual bias. The w stands for will and the o for opportunity.) In an organisation of any size, these may be different individuals or a variety of committees. Miller and Heiman (1989) have identified the following key prospect roles in the buying process:

- the user(s) of the service;

- the technical buyer, whose approval is needed, acting as a gatekeeper;

- the economic buyer, whose authority is needed to release the funds.

It is difficult – if not impossible – to identify these from outside, and so the fourth role, that of coach, is important. The coach is the member of the prospect organisation who is committed to your consultancy's offering and who can provide guidance to (and perhaps influence over) those filling the other key roles.

If you have immediate access to a powerful chief executive, then this distinction of role is less relevant. In other cases you need to recognise the roles, and the buying process that will be engaged. For example, the situation where a client has been commissioned by his board to carry out a study of IT requirements for his business is a quite different selling process from trying to sell a study on IT to a client who is satisfied with his present arrangements. An important objective early in the sales process is therefore to obtain intelligence about the buying process and the roles of the interested parties. This will enable you to focus your selling effort to best effect.

Approaching the prospect

It is an unusual prospect who would engage management consultants without first meeting them – and an unusual firm of consultants who would agree to work with a client under these conditions. So meetings are an essential part of the selling process (see Figure 4.2). The purpose of the approach is therefore to secure a selling meeting, preferably with the MAN (who, of course, could be a woman!). You may need to do some preliminary research on who might be the MAN, and telephonists and secretaries can be helpful in guiding you to the right person. In situations of any complexity, it may be necessary to identify a coach (see above) as a first step.

Next, you have to decide how you will approach the prospect. Should you telephone and ask for an appointment, or do you need to warm him or her up with a letter beforehand? Part of the promotional activity of larger consultancies is to circulate their own promotional literature, such as newsletters or business journals to prospective clients. This means that there will already be some awareness among prospects about the firm and its services. If this is the case, then there may be no need to warm up with a letter beforehand.

Consultants' publicity material may have some sort of response mechanism built in (eg a tear-off slip that can be returned to register interest). This means that if approaches are focused on those who have shown interest, a better conversion ratio should result.

The objective in warming up the prospect is to provide enough information to convince him or her of the benefits of investing time in a telephone conversation, and to warm towards the idea of meeting you. You are seeking, in fact, to satisfy the qualification process on the prospect's side. If your service can be explained and understood in a simple telephone conversation, this might be the best method of qualification. If it is complicated, or you feel uncomfortable at a direct approach, then writing a letter might be best. You have also to consider what you are offering at the first meeting – what benefits will accrue to the prospect in meeting you. Many executives are prepared to make time to see consultants speculatively, but rarely simply to hear them give a catalogue of their services. They need to know how the consultancy's services are going to develop business performance and competitiveness, or remedy problems. Sometimes consultants may offer an appraisal of (some aspect of) the business early in the relationship as an incentive. For example, a strategy consultancy might make a presentation on a business's position within its sector, hoping to display a knowledge and capability that will persuade the prospect to do business with them.

If the presentation is to be effective, then the consultancy has to invest time in preparing it. Time should not be invested lightly, and the selling team should feel that it is spreading its seed on fertile ground. The presentation is therefore unlikely to be the first meeting between consultancy and prospect.

Comments on telephone technique

Although telephone technique is a basic selling skill, it is one in which I have often found experienced consultants to be weak. The following notes are therefore intended to summarise the key points.

One of the first challenges is getting through to speak to executives at a prospect. If they are warmed up and expecting you to call, then there is less difficulty. Even so, it can be difficult to find a time when the executive is free to speak to you. As a salesperson you will want to keep the initiative and therefore will want to make the call yourself. If there is little incentive for a prospect to call back, it is unlikely he or she will do so. You have to make the call at times when you are free, so you need to know when the executive is likely to be free to receive it. It is best to avoid the core times for meetings – 10 am–12 am and 2 pm–4 pm. Some consultants try to phone before 9 am or after 6 pm, because they might also avoid a protective secretary at those times. Even so, my rule of thumb is that it takes an *average* of three telephone calls before you can get to speak to a prospect.

Secretaries are more often helpful than obstructive; ideally, you should make the prospect's secretary your ally in the selling process. Occasionally one might be too protective, asking your business and judging that it is unlikely to be of interest to the boss. If it really is impossible to get past the secretary, or enlist her help, you can:

- abandon this prospect – invest your time in others that might offer a better chance of a sale;

- try to bypass the secretary. You need to be convinced of the error of her judgement. Moreover, it could be embarrassing to end up talking to her again despite trying to bypass her;

- find a different point of access. This could be via another executive in the same organisation, seeking an introduction through a mutual acquaintance, or aiming to 'bump into' the executive or an appropriate connector at some business or social function.

A secretary can be helpful in easing communication if the executive is proving inaccessible. A comment from the consultant might be: 'I wrote to Mr Smith last week concerning our services, which we thought might be of particular value to your business at this time. In my letter I said I'd phone to see whether we might meet, and to fix a mutually convenient time'. In my experience, the secretary's response might be:

- 'Yes, he's asked me to fix a meeting when you rang.' (Great!).

- 'He asked me to tell you that he's not interested.'

- 'He's not spoken to me about it.'

In the last case you might then ask the secretary to find out what the boss wants to do, so that if he or she is not available next time you ring, at least you can stop wasting time if they are not interested. But this is very much a fall-back position if you can't get hold of the boss in the first place.

Prepare for the call

Before placing the call, you have to have prepared what the structure of the telephone conversation is going to be. Preparing what you are going to say is only half the telephone conversation. What are you aiming to find out, as well as to convey, in this conversation? You will want to confirm your understanding of the prospect's needs, the position of your contact in the buying process, and the next steps, at the very least. This is to enable you to qualify the prospect for the next stage.

Have fall-back objectives

There is a series of possible outcomes from a telephone approach:

- receive an invitation to tender;
- fix a meeting with the prospect;
- a meeting is to be arranged at some future date;
- send material then contact again;
- call back at a specified time in future;
- no interest.

The best outcome is that you get an invitation to tender – ie the prospect has an immediate need for your services. You will want to qualify this, ie you are unlikely to put in a proposal without first meeting the prospect.

Next best is that the prospect agrees to a meeting; you have achieved your objective in the telephone approach. The remaining outcomes are of decreasing commercial attractiveness. The reason for listing them, however, is to show that the outcome is not a simple 'yes/no' to a meeting. Even if there is no interest in your services now, you may have created a link that brings a prospective client into your network – a link you could probably nurture and exercise profitably at some time in the future.

CONDUCTING SALES MEETINGS

Having got access to your target prospect, the next step is to try to persuade the prospect to invite you to tender for a piece of consultancy work. This is accomplished by conducting one or a series of sales meetings.

The initial meeting

Of these meetings, the most important is the initial contact made with each person involved in the buying process: you never get a second chance to make a first impression. Better selling performance derives from stacking the odds in your own favour. If you can make a better first impression, then you will have a better chance of winning the sale. The first meeting will have a profound effect on what follows, which is why this is the one on which we will concentrate. Obviously all the others will have some impact, but they will only modify the impression created at the first. Moreover, the first meeting will be significant, as that will be largely instrumental in defining the general areas in which client and consultancy are to work together.

There are thus two critical dimensions to the initial meeting:

- the effect it has on the relationship;

- its contribution to defining the consultancy project.

The two are related; for example, the salesperson who catechises a senior executive to identify the focus of a project may damage the relationship. The relationship dimension is crucial. Any meeting with a client will affect the relationship with the consultant, and so meetings must have a relationship objective as well as one of content. As indicated in Chapter 3, it may be better not to make a sale but to win a worthwhile relationship, rather than the opposite.

So in this section we concentrate on the initial meeting.

Preparation

Most consultants will nod vigorously when asked, 'Should you prepare for a sales meeting?', but will disagree on what form that preparation should take.

If Wittreich's third criterion is to be satisfied – 'buying the professional' – the consultancy salesperson has to be more than simply a broker of useful resources; you have to show the value of the connection between the needs of the prospect's business and the services of the consultancy – for example, how your services will help the prospect address current key business issues. But again, as in the telephone conversation, you must avoid a preoccupation with what you are going to say. There is more extensive comment on the agenda for the first meeting below; for now, you should consider what you need to find out from the prospect, as well as what to say. The quality of questions and comments can serve either to impress the prospect – or quite the opposite.

You need to consider whether you need to take something along to the first meeting. One of my associates recommends that at the very least you take a typewritten sheet with a list of points for discussion – not necessarily as formal as an agenda – to the first meeting. The aim is to show that you have given some thought to this particular meeting – it is not a clone of a score of similar meetings you have conducted over the previous months.

Personal impact

The salesperson in consultancy is initially the embodiment of the product. In selling a tangible item, it can be described and displayed. Not so in consultancy: the prospect will imbue the consultancy service with the characteristics of the salesperson.

Consultants learn early in their careers how to dress properly, how to relate to clients and how to manage their body language. These requirements are as relevant to selling as they are to consultancy. It is important to recognise that people take in information through what they see, hear and feel, and use all three channels. People have preferences (I am conscious of a personal bias to visual communication), so each salesperson will have his or her own preference. The danger is that you will then use that channel exclusively; this will be all right with clients who have the same preference, but less effective with those whose preference is different. So you need to consider visual aids, the words you use, and the rapport you generate with the prospect.

Opening the meeting

For those new to selling, there is a problem about what to say after the initial pleasantries. Table 4.1 suggests an outline agenda for an initial meeting.

As with meeting anybody for the first time, a meeting will open with pleasantries, to start building a personal relationship. Get the prospect talking early on; because you have an agenda doesn't mean you have to do all the talking! There then needs to be a natural bridge to talking

Table 4.1 *Outline agenda for an initial meeting*

1. Pleasantries
2. Bridge to the business discussion
3. Probing for prospects' concerns
4. Discussing how these concerns might be jointly addressed
5. Decide next steps

about business. This needs to be done by body language as well as orally. Opening your briefcase and bringing out your pad and pen will serve to show that the business of the meeting is going to start.

Some years ago, I had reached this point in my first meeting with a finance director of a prospective client, to whom I had been introduced by the personnel manager, who reported to him. I had some previous discussions with the personnel manager who, I assumed, had briefed the FD. We then commenced the meeting and I proceeded on from the discussions I had had with the personnel manager. After about 15 minutes, the FD stopped and said, 'Hang on a minute; what are we talking about here? I'm lost.' The personnel manager had not briefed him, and that was the last meeting I had with that prospect. With that experience behind me, I favour a recap on the background to the meeting as an introduction to the business discussion. This serves to make sure that both you and the prospect are starting from the same point.

A technique that salespeople are sometimes taught is to 'take control' of a meeting. What this means in practice is controlling the agenda. Personally as a prospect, I'm not sure I want to be controlled. The prospect will be coming to the sales meeting with an agenda – even if it is not articulated. The good salesperson will allow for the fact that the prospect has an agenda and will let him or her express it. So you will perhaps wish to agree on what you are going to cover. If it is a first meeting, it is helpful for you and your prospect each to give a brief summary of your business and where you fit into it.

These first items on the agenda are relatively uncontentious and will serve to help build rapport. Next you have to start to probe for the prospect's concerns and show how your services relate to them. (The probing pyramid technique, set out below, can be used for structuring this part of the meeting.) Finally, as shown in Table 4.1, you have to agree on the next steps to be taken by both sides following the meeting, which ideally should take the selling process on to the next stage.

The probing pyramid: how to establish the prospect's needs

It can be difficult to decide what questions to ask. What do you need to know? What kind of questioning should you use?

I am indebted to my associate, Dennis Sobey, for introducing me to the concept of the 'probing pyramid' which helps to identify the prospect's needs. Although a simple model, it can provide the basis for an extensive discussion. Once the probing pyramid is understood and put into action, it provides you with both the types of question to ask and the order in which they might be asked, as the meeting – or a series of meetings – progresses. It is particularly useful in planning the first meeting with a new prospect. The framework is shown in Figure 4.3.

The sequence of the agenda is shown on the right. At the start you may discuss facts about the business, but then you need to move on to the issues affecting the business. There are two potential traps at this stage, in that it is tempting:

- having identified one issue, then to proceed with the next stages. At an initial meeting, if you are to identify other relevant issues, note

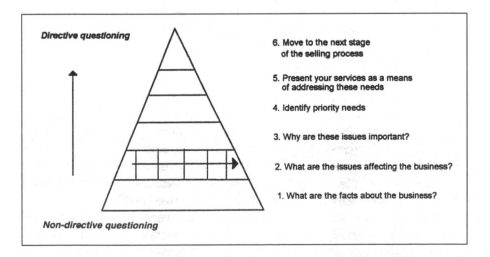

Figure 4.3 *The probing pyramid*

each issue, and then remain at item 2 in the agenda until you have exhausted this topic;

- to leap straight from item 2 to item 5 without going through items 3 and 4. These items enable you to focus your response in item 5 in a way that will be attractive to the prospect.

Framing questions

Questioning must not, of course, be an interrogation! Happily, however, most people like to talk about their business if asked properly. As the questioning progresses, you gradually move from the use of non-directive to directive questions. You may also find that the focus of the questioning changes – eg from dealing with one small part of the organisation to issues affecting the organisation as a whole. Use open-ended questions to broaden the discussion. These are the questions that typically begin with Who, What, Why, When, How, Where?

Directive questions are the questions prefaced Would, Could, Should, Will, Is, If, May, Can? They restrict the response to a yes/no answer. They help to check your understanding of the information that has been elicited by the open-ended questions.

In both cases, the pressure of silence may encourage the prospect to open up. What is equally true is that if you are talking, the prospect is not. You need to encourage the prospect by your questioning to give you the information you require. Of course, people will give information in response not only to questions. An assertion or a comment may also elicit a response. (Listen to any popular radio or TV news programme to hear examples of these being used.)

Face-to-face skills

Thus far we have considered the content of the initial meeting. Here are some tips on handling the meeting.

- You will be better able to deal with a meeting effectively if you are calm. I remember attending an initial meeting with an experienced colleague some years ago. We had to climb to the second floor of the office block, and I noticed that my colleague was climbing even more slowly than his senior years required. The reason, he explained, was that he should not reach the client's office out of breath.

You will be more stressed at the start of a meeting if you are late, and you will also create an unfavourable initial impression. The rule is always to arrive in good time, with a margin allowed for delays.

- Listen, and show by your body language that you are doing so. Nod encouragingly, ask questions, and take notes, to do this. Encourage the other person to talk.

  There will be clients who are verbose or who stray into irrelevancies; bring them back to the topic with a question. You can interrupt without giving offence by saying, 'I wonder if I might interrupt you at this point to ask ...?'

- Use evaluative or descriptive statements in your questioning, rather than judgemental ones. For example, don't ask, 'Why has your division failed to meet its profit targets?' Better to ask, 'Why has your division had difficulties in meeting its profit targets?' People will more happily admit to difficulties than failure. The trick is to talk of half-full bottles rather than half-empty ones. (Of course, there are occasions when you will wish to confront a client by using judgemental statements, but this should be by design rather than accident.)

- When questioning, vary the pace. One question rapidly following the last quickly begins to sound like an interrogation. A pause will also serve to show that you are listening.

- Avoid asking double questions; this can be confusing and, most probably you will get answers only to one of the questions. A double question is of the sort, 'Have things been so difficult in previous years? Do you see an upturn for next year?'

- Another trap is turning open-ended questions into multiple choice close-ended ones. For example, 'How do you see the future prospects for your business? Will competition increase? Or will there be a general recovery in the sector?' The open-ended question has been lost, and the consultant is leading the client.

Team selling

In order to satisfy Wittreich's third criterion, it may be sensible for more than one consultant to attend the sales meeting. Whenever there is more than one consultant attending a meeting with a client – whether it is the first or a subsequent meeting – it is important that you have worked out your respective roles. You should have decided how you are to position yourselves with the client. If the aim is that one of you is to be the leader of the project, if it is sold, then that person must be allowed to establish their credentials with the client.

At the very least, you should decide which of you is to lead the discussion at the meeting. The person who leads should make openings for the other to make a contribution – it doesn't help the selling process to be fighting over air time. It is also incumbent on the person in the secondary role to respond to the openings provided by the leader. Some years ago, I was in a sales role and took along a technical expert to meet a prospect. I kept on making opportunities for him to contribute – passing the conversation over to him with comments like 'Wouldn't you say that was the case?', but he refused to respond. It was like serving tennis balls to someone who made not the slightest effort to return them. Eventually, the prospect got tired of this and asked me, 'Who's this then – your pet parrot?' That was the last meeting with that prospect.

Managing the selling process

Early in the selling process you will need to judge how much work – eg how many meetings – is required to win an invitation to tender. In some circumstances the opportunity may arise at the first meeting; this will be the case when your consultancy offering is clearly defined and you have carefully pre-qualified the prospect. For example, a recruitment consultant may have established the prospect's need for recruitment services during a preliminary telephone call. At the initial meeting the consultant will have sold the firm's services extrinsically, so that the prospect feels encouraged to invite the consultant to submit a proposal if there is a vacancy to be filled. In other cases a series of meetings may be required, to do one or more of the following:

- clarify the nature of the consulting project;
- meet others of the client staff who might be involved in the buying process;
- introduce others from the consultancy to help in selling or who might be involved in operating the project.

The criteria described in Chapter 2 are useful to remember in the sales process, viz:

- The client has to recognise that a problem or opportunity exists.

- The client has to believe that it merits attention.

- The client must believe that it is possible to resolve the problem or realise the opportunity.

- The client must see the value of outside consultancy help.

- The client must want your help.

Remember that it is a competitive market. As well as managing your side of the sales process, you need to convince the prospect that yours is the right consultancy to undertake the project.

WINNING THE SALE

Having been invited to tender for a piece of consultancy work, the final stage in the selling process is to turn this into an actual sale. Almost without exception, a written proposal will be required; this may need to be supported by a face-to-face presentation to the prospect. Other activities may also be required to nurse the sale at this stage.

Preparing a proposal

Whatever the selling or buying process being conducted, it is good practice to submit a written proposal, so that both you and the client have shared expectations of what is to be done. The question of what to include in a proposal is dealt with in Chapter 5; herein we deal with the sales context.

The function of the proposal may vary from being simply a record of what has already been orally agreed, to being the document on which the client is to make the buying decision. Some proposals may need to set out the rationale for carrying out the project in the first place (ie the need for it and the benefits of proceeding). This is required when, for example, the client or the client's colleagues need to be reassured of the benefits of proceeding with the project. If this is not required, then you need only to describe how you will meet the needs defined by the client, and the reasons why your consultancy practice is particularly well suited so to do.

In taking the decision on what to include in your proposal, you need to consider the probable audience. What can they be safely assumed to know already? If in doubt, it is probably better to include explanatory material, rather than leave it out. Ideally, the proposal should serve to confirm that which has already been agreed, but it should also bring some added value to the client.

Some years ago, I and some associates were commissioning a piece of consultancy, and our experience is instructive. We interviewed four firms. With one, the meeting was curtailed; the consultant made some disparaging remarks about a couple of our competitors. My associate asked for us to be excused for a moment. Outside the meeting he said, 'We can't possibly use him. What if he were to make similar remarks about us?' So we found an excuse to end the meeting.

A second consultant came from a large firm. Being ourselves a small firm, we had an uncomfortable (and possibly unfounded) feeling that we would not be treated with great importance, because of our size.

We were left with two contenders, both of whom we invited to put in proposals. One firm, (Firm A), although we were not very taken with them at the outset, conducted a very good sales meeting; by the end, they were front-runners. Then we received their proposals.

Firm A sent in a proposal that simply confirmed the assignment. It seemed very much like a boilerplate job – ie a standard proposal that had received some limited tailoring to meet our requirements. By contrast, the other firm in the running – Firm B – produced a thoughtful proposal that really added value. It showed an appreciation of our circumstances, and contributed helpfully to our thinking, which gave us greater confidence in their ability to do the job. Had Firm A produced something half as good, they would have got the job; as it was, Firm B won the contract.

The message therefore is that you should seek opportunities to add value in a proposal. This can be by an insightful appraisal of a client's situation, helping the client to gain a clearer understanding of the circumstances in which you are going to deliver your consultancy services.

Sometimes it may be possible (and helpful) to prepare a proposal in draft and send this for comment to a close contact in the client organisation involved in the buying process (such as the 'coach', described earlier). It can then be refined to meet the client's needs more closely. (This can be part of a sophisticated selling technique: by getting the client's involvement in producing the proposal, it is seen as a joint problem-solving process rather than selling.) You also need to know what other opportunities you might have for selling the proposal – eg the production of an executive summary, or a presentation.

Your approach should be tailored to the buying process used by the client. You need to know how the buying decision is to be taken, and the factors on which it is to be made. People who haven't met you can judge you only by your proposal, whereas a presentation to an audience of decision-makers or influencers can help in building their confidence and reducing their sense of uncertainty.

Nursing the sale

Once the proposal has been submitted, the sale will need to be nursed. It is rarely satisfactory to submit a proposal and then wait for a 'yes/no' answer. Ideally the salesperson should know the steps involved in the client's decision-making process and be on hand to deal with any difficulties and to direct attention to the benefits of your undertaking the assignment.

Other than meetings, useful actions that the salesperson might take are to contact the prospect to:

- check that the proposal has been received;

- get initial reactions – likes/worries, etc, and confirm the decision-making process;

- identify any real difficulties the client has in choosing your proposal.

On this last point, note that in the private sector particularly, price is only one of several factors that influence a client's buying decision. Classic negotiation on the cost, payment terms and so on may be required, but these are less important than that the prospect should:

- believe that you have clearly understood their needs;

- have confidence in the consultancy's people;

- believe that the proposed approach will achieve the benefits claimed.

If a client is unhappy with a proposal, therefore, see this as a joint problem-solving process. The client needs consultancy, you want to provide it – so how can this be done to the best advantage of all concerned? When a client expresses concern, the salesperson must probe to find out what that concern really is. For example, suppose your estimate of the consultancy fees for a particular job is £20,000, and the client is resistant to this. Let's assume that your fee estimate is based on a costing of fee days times fee rate. An obvious option is to attempt to reduce the fees. If, however, your fee rate is realistic and your estimate of the time required is accurate, then reducing the total fee means changing one of these elements.

The general practice within consultancy firms is to set fee rates annually – or more frequently – at a fixed rate for costing purposes. In this environment, this means that a reduction in total fees will show up as a 'loss' – ie the same number of days at a lower fee rate than standard. The upshot is that there is then some pressure to do the job more quickly, or to use less expensive resources – both of which are likely to diminish quality. So, go back to the original problem: why does the client want to reduce the fees? Is it because they do not think it represents value for money? Or is it because they do not have the budget?

If their reservations are about value for money, do you as their consultant truly believe that the benefits of this project adequately outweigh the costs – both actual and opportunity costs? If you do, then the problem is one of communication. The client:

- does not recognise the benefits; or

- does not value the benefits in the same way as you; or

- lacks the confidence that the benefits will accrue.

In these circumstances there is a major job to be done to diagnose which of these applies and then to take remedial action. Of course, if the benefits are not truly worthwhile, should you be advising them to proceed with the project in the first place?

If the client's problem concerns their budget, can the budget be changed? If the answer is no, the onus is on you to see what you can do to restructure the project within the time allowed by a reduced budget, usually by reducing the scope. I find an effective strategy is to go through this with the client. We go through the tasks and the estimate of times required for each, to see what can be pared. This allows the client to make suggestions that may not have occurred to me, as well as making clear what the effect of the reduced budget will be.

Losing the sale

Not every bid will succeed, but don't lose heart! If you have been sufficiently impressive, you will be invited to be on the tender list for the next piece of consultancy that comes along for that client. Anyhow, a good bid should cement the client relationship, and provide the basis for further discussion about what you have to offer in other areas of consultancy.

DEVELOPING SELLING SKILLS

Whether you win or lose a sale, you should carefully analyse the reasons for the outcome, and apply the lessons to future sales efforts (the process shown in Figure 4.4). They may be surprising; for example, one consultancy won a job and asked, 'Why us?' It emerged that one reason for their success was that they used colour slides in their presentation! The client interpreted the investment in more expensive colour as a significant commitment to the project.

Getting better at selling may mean doing different things, or doing things differently. The virtuous circle of improvement shown in

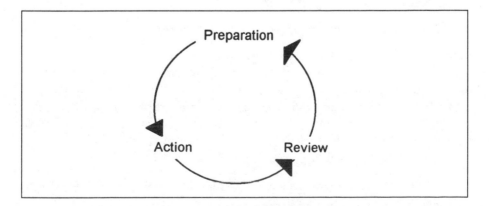

Figure 4.4 *The virtuous circle of improving selling skills*

Figure 4.4 is helpful in thinking about how to do this.

Although the focus in selling is on action, it has to be preceded by careful preparation. After action, you review how things have gone, so that your preparation will be better informed next time. All three steps need to be carried out carefully to improve performance.

MONITORING SALES PERFORMANCE

Monitoring sales performance is important for two reasons:

- It shows what the level of future sales is likely to be, and where sales effort needs to be directed.

- Successful sales performance can be analysed to identify the reasons for success, and hence provide a guide to good practice.

For the purposes of monitoring sales performance a client can be allocated to stages in the selling process as follows:

- *Sales development*   When sales activities are aimed at developing a relationship with the client, but there is no specific project in view.

- *Prospect*   Where there is a specific project (or projects) in view, but for which the practice has not yet received a request for a proposal or invitation to tender from the client.

- *Proposal*   A proposal has been submitted to the client that the practice should carry out a specific project.

- *Sale*   When the client has accepted a proposal.

The steps in selling as defined above are set out in Figure 4.5.

As well as clients arising from sales development, prospects and proposals may derive from *direct enquiries*. There will also be clients lost at each stage (called *turn-downs*) because, for example, of the absence of a suitable project, the deferral or cancellation of a project, or a contract that is awarded to a competing provider of consultancy services.

Sales performance will be measured by:

- the volume of business (number of clients, value of projects, etc) at each stage in the sales process;

- the conversion of business from one stage to the next.

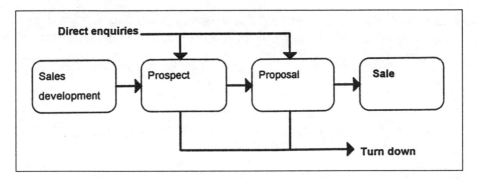

Figure 4.5 *Steps in selling*

To this end, sales activity needs to be monitored, and examples of the type of information that can be recorded are shown in Figures 4.6–4.8. This shows the information on a form, but it is more normal to keep the data on a computer data base. These records should be completed regularly. Their layout means that the status of the sales process to a client can be assessed quickly, and action taken to follow up where required.

Sales development record

Sales development is the development of a relationship with a potential client, targeted as being a likely buyer of your services. It should be the responsibility of a salesperson assigned to that target. A sales development record is shown on Figure 4.6. It takes some time to develop clients in this category into prospects, and it is easy to let this category get too small. You should therefore review on a regular basis whether the level of activity in this category is sufficient.

Prospects record

Prospects can arise from either clients out of the sales development process or direct enquiries. Every client for whom you are currently undertaking projects should also be regarded as a prospective client.

The record in Figure 4.7 has spaces for the project for which the salesperson hopes the client will issue an invitation to tender, the likely revenue and an estimate of the probability that a sale will indeed follow. A separate calculation can then be made of the sum of the probable revenues. Actual sales often turn out to be different, but this figure gives a measure of the probable sales in the pipeline. This can be used as an indicator of possible future peaks and troughs of sales, which would have implications for revenue and resource utilisation.

Proposals record

The record in Figure 4.8 is similar to the prospects form, except that only firm proposals are recorded. Here, the sum of the probable sales is a good measure of future workload. Points to monitor particularly on this record include:

- a high-value proposal of low probability that will place a high demand on resources if it should sell;

- a low total probable revenue combined with high probabilities which is a sign that future workload might be low if the probabilities have been over-estimated.

Other uses

It is important to monitor the conversion rate from one stage to the next. Key ratios to monitor are:

- $\dfrac{\text{No of sales}}{\text{No of proposals}}$

- $\dfrac{\text{Value of sales}}{\text{Value of proposals}}$

Typically in management consultancy these figures might be one-third to a half – ie only one in two or three proposals are accepted. If the ratio becomes too low, this can be a sign that either you are bidding for the wrong business, or that your proposals are insufficiently competitive. Likewise, a high conversion rate might indicate opportunities for business expansion. Reasons for proposals being turned down should be monitored so that conversion performance can be improved.

Of course, the records need to be kept up to date. This means being honest about those prospects who show no sign of turning into business. It is a matter of judgement which clients should remain on the Sales Development and Prospects records. You may wish to remove a prospective client from the sales records if the likelihood of any revenue deriving from the effort is low.

Last updated:

Account Manager	Client	Current position	Next action	By when

Figure 4.6 *Sales development record*

Last updated:

Account manager	Client	Possible project	Likely revenue	Proba-bility	Current position	Next action	By when

Figure 4.7 *Prospects record*

Last updated:

Account manager	Client	Project	Value	Proba-bility	Current position, competition etc.	Next action	By when

Figure 4.8 *Proposals record*

Finally, use these sales records as a basis for the process of improvement shown in Figure 4.4. Review performance to find out what techniques are successful, and which clients are the best bet. Distinguish successful performance from unsuccessful, and so build up an understanding of what constitutes good selling practice for your consultancy firm.

5
COMMERCIAL ASPECTS OF CONSULTANCY

A former colleague once explained his view of consultancy thus: 'We are in the business of selling people their dreams,' he said. 'Consultants are the dream merchants of business.' This may be the case, but dreams turn into nightmares when consultants promise the unattainable to a client. At the best they will have a damaged reputation; in these increasingly litigious times, they may end up being sued.

All that a client buys on purchasing an assignment is a promise; unlike the – say – car salesman, a consultancy salesperson cannot point to the product and say, 'This is what you're going to get.' It is therefore essential that both client and consultant have a clear idea of the commercial transaction in which they are engaged, which is embodied in the terms of reference and terms of business.

The phrase 'terms of reference' will be interpreted variously by different consultants. The *Shorter Oxford Dictionary* defines terms of reference as 'the terms which define the scope of an inquiry', and this is a good starting point. Like Humpty Dumpty in *Through the Looking Glass*, however, in this chapter I shall define it to mean what I want it to mean. In my definition, as we shall see, the terms of reference are enlarged to cover the 'how' and 'why' of the assignment, as well as the deliverables at its conclusion.

Whereas terms of reference in this definition relate to the *content* of a project, terms of business will relate to the commercial *context*. For a consultancy firm, the major element of concern in terms of business will be the payments they receive from clients. In this chapter, therefore, we consider the basis on which a consultancy project is costed, as well as the terms of payment. We shall also look at other methods of generating revenue in consultancy.

All these aspects are brought together in a proposal submitted to the client. The proposal is the basis of the contract between consultant and client; it provides the foundation for all that follows within a consultancy project. It lays out the mutual expectations of the client and consultant – an important aspect of managing the client relationship (see Chapter 9).

A FRAMEWORK FOR ESTABLISHING TERMS OF REFERENCE

Terms of reference need to be established clearly for every assignment. Usually they should be written to avoid misunderstandings but, as with any contract, they can be oral as well as written. Figure 5.1 shows the framework for developing terms of reference. It consists of:

- client objectives;

- assignment objectives;

- the assignment plan.

These three relate together in a hierarchy of objectives; to go up the hierarchy, you ask 'Why?'; thus:

- Why are we carrying out this plan?
  — To achieve the assignment objectives.

- Why are we aiming at these assignment objectives?
  — To help the client achieve his objectives.

To go down the hierarchy, you ask 'How?', so:

- How are the client's objectives to be achieved?
  — Through achieving the assignment objectives.

- How are the assignment objectives to be achieved?
  — By means of the plan.

It is worth noting that usually there is only one answer to the question 'Why?', whereas there may be several answers to the question 'How?'. What this means is that the consultancy assignment may be only one of

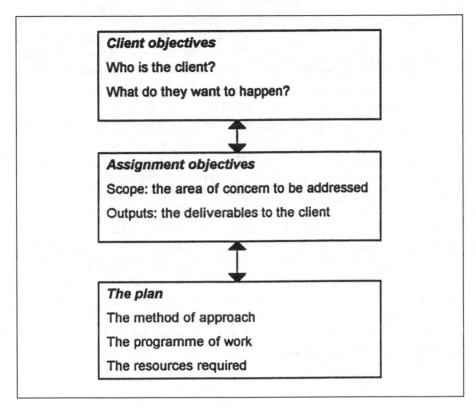

Figure 5.1 *Terms of reference*

several contributors to the client's objectives. The others, however, may not require consultancy support, nor necessarily be in hand. In the following sections we consider each of these three elements comprising terms of reference.

The client's objectives

Consultants have to remember that their work is only a means to an end from the client's point of view. A consultant is (rightly) means-oriented, whereas his or her client is ends-oriented. A consultant sees an assignment as a series of tasks, whereas a typical client sees it as a series of deliverables. But you should never lose sight of the commercial context in which you are carrying out the assignment. To this end, you must remain aware who the client is and what the client wants to happen. This can sometimes be difficult when you are engrossed in the minutiae of a complex assignment. (Or, as the old adage has it, 'When you're up to your ass in crocodiles, it's hard to remember you're there to drain the swamp!')

It is essential to know who the real client is. If we call the person who is dealing with the consultant the 'sponsor' of the assignment, it is important to know if the sponsor is the real client, or if there is someone behind the sponsor who is pushing to carry out the project. In the ICC case study in Chapter 1 (pp.18–19), for example, the sponsor for a consultancy project is the general manager (GM). What we do not (yet) know is whether John Smith's visit is at the GM's initiative or whether the GM has been pushed into this by a superior. Were the latter true, then this might have a fundamental influence on the GM's attitude to the project; would he, for example, be a reluctant client? If this were the case, John Smith might find the assignment more difficult – the GM might be unwilling to release resources, make his own time available, and so on. What the client wants can be considered at two levels – personal and commercial objectives.

Commercial objectives

These will relate ultimately to:

- improving the performance of the business;
- improving its competitive position;
- developing new business.

Obviously the client's objectives for a particular assignment may not be phrased in these terms; nevertheless, it can be helpful to consultant and client alike to make explicit the causality between the commercial objective as framed, and those stated above. This is easy to do in the case of ICC: the client wants to reduce product costs so that the company's competitive position and profitability improve.

But what of assignments that are related less directly to commercial objectives – for example, carrying out a job evaluation assignment, helping with an office relocation, or delivering a training course? In these cases, tracking the client's objectives back to see how they relate to commercial objectives should help fashion the assignment so that it is more helpful to the client.

Personal objectives

These are equally relevant. The assignment sponsor will like the assignment to help him or her to do the job better, to run a better, more efficient department or business, to redound to his or her credit, and so on. Equally, the sponsor will want to be sure the assignment doesn't go wrong and is not seen as an expensive waste of time. For this latter reason, a key dimension of a consultant's early contact with a sponsor is confidence building (see Chapter 9).

So there are general objectives that we can ascribe to the client at the start of an assignment. There may also be specific ones. The consultancy salesperson may have to probe to find these. 'What are the client's unwritten objectives?' should be an item on the checklist of points that the salesperson ought to cover. There may be other requirements in terms of the conduct of the assignment:

- the extent to which the sponsor is to be involved in the detail;
- freedom of access to other parts of the organisation (does everything have to be cleared through the sponsor?);
- his or her wish to be involved in helping you in the development of ideas (eg does the sponsor want to be used as a sounding board, or to receive considered views only?)

All this is about setting and understanding expectations, which affects the client relationship. You need to establish a sound *modus operandi* with the client, which means understanding them personally as well as in their business role.

The assignment objectives

In Figure 5.1, the assignment objectives are defined by scope and output:

- the *scope* defines the areas of concern that are to be addressed;
- the *output* is what the client is going to get in respect of each of these areas – the deliverables.

Obviously these two together define the amount of work that an assignment might involve. The broader the scope, then the greater the amount of work that may be involved. Definition of the deliverables is equally important, particularly because they reflect the depth of analysis that is required to meet them. An in-depth study may need ten times the work of a 'quick and dirty' review.

It is essential that the consultancy and the client have the same view of these two items. A deadly sin in consultancy is to put yourself in a position where you have to do free consultancy because you have overrun your budget. This happens when a client has been promised a deliverable which the consultancy has not achieved within the given budget, or when there has been a misunderstanding over the scope of the assignment. Additional resources are therefore required to accomplish the output required.

If you find it difficult to define the scope of the assignment, then you are probably having to deal with a 'messy' problem. Some preliminary work may therefore be required in order for the scope to be defined. The assignment, therefore, has to be broken into phases, the output of each phase defining the scope for the next. This is exemplified in Table 5.1. which shows the scope and deliverables for the different levels in consultancy assignments that were defined in Chapter 1.

For example, in the ICC case study, we assume that the objective of reducing high product costs has already been agreed, so there is no need to start at level 1. At level 2, John Smith has to verify what the causes of

Table 5.1 *Scope and output for each level of intervention*

Level	Scope	Output
1	Sense of organisational malaise	Purposes defined
2	How to achieve the purposes	Main issues that relate to achievement of purposes identified
3	How to resolve defined issues	How they can be best resolved
4	Implementation	Solutions put in place

high product costs might be – based on the clues he has found during his initial tour. At the end of the work at this level he should have identified the issues causing high product costs; the level 3 intervention would be to decide how these might be best resolved.

At the start John Smith can only guess what solutions need to be implemented to reduce production costs. The terms of reference, therefore, cannot be comprehensive – he cannot prescribe (other than in the most general terms) what the outcome of the level 3 intervention will be, because the outputs of level 2 set the scope for level 3. He can therefore give firm terms of reference only for his work at level 2. The client, may, however, require an estimate of fees for work from identifying the issues through to implementing the solutions. How to deal with this dilemma is dealt with below under 'What do we tell the client?' (pp.110–13).

The second element of assignment objectives shown in Figure 5.1 is outputs. Outputs are the deliverables of the assignment. The rules for specifying outputs are:

- Make sure that each item identified within the scope has an output associated with it. An item in the scope with no output raises the question, 'How are you going to address this for the client?' An output unrelated to the scope usually implies that:
    - the output is related to part of the scope that has not been articulated, in which case the scope should be revised;
    - the output is not required (for example, a consultant may produce an assignment report that is primarily for consumption within the consultancy practice instead of being a material means of advancing the performance of the client), in which case you should consider not producing the output.

- Try to define outputs in terms which show how they relate to the client's objectives. 'So what?' analysis can be helpful here – ask 'So what?' of each output, to see whether it relates to the client objective. (This is particularly useful when you are tempted to produce outputs consisting only of data feedback.)

Table 5.2 shows the scope and outputs for ICC for interventions at level 2 and 3.

At the start of his assignment, John Smith has accepted the purpose that product costs have to be reduced, but can only guess what areas

Table 5.2 *Assignment objectives*

Level	Scope	Outputs
2	How can production costs be reduced?	The major issues resulting in high product costs identified
3	Wastage and rework rates	Report on how to reduce them
	Machine downtime	Recommend improved maintenance schedule
	Customer expectations of product quality	Recommended changes to product specifications
	Suppliers' prices	Recommendations on improved purchasing policies and procedures

need to be tackled to reduce them. At the end of the level 2 intervention, therefore, his output is a more focused view of the areas that might be investigated in more detail.

Suppose that at the end of this intervention he has identified the items shown in Table 5.2 as the issues causing high product costs. At the next level of intervention (level 3) the deliverables could be the reports and recommendations shown in the figure. If he were then to help the client with a level 4 intervention, he would support the implementation of his recommendations.

I used to be worried that the output that a consultant produces so often consists of reports and recommendations – hardly a direct intervention into the client environment. But given that a consultant rarely has executive authority within a client, outputs for action or a decision are usually expressed in terms of recommendations. Of course, the skill of the consultant lies in not only making the recommendations, but also in getting them accepted. (See Chapter 8.)

Although consultants can forecast *outputs*, they should be more conservative when forecasting *outcomes* or results. If the consultancy has total control over the factors influencing outcomes, then they can be more confident of predicting what the results of an assignment might be.

Usually, however, a consultancy assignment is a joint activity between consultant and client, and so the results will depend on the cooperation and skill of the client staff, and the vagaries of the business environment. For these reasons, it is unusual for a consultancy to be able to guarantee the results of an assignment in terms of – say – decreased costs or increased performance. If it were rash enough to do so, and the expected results were not achieved, the client might reasonably claim some sort of redress.

What is most helpful under these circumstances is for the consultancy to indicate conditionally what the outcomes might be. 'Given the co-operation of your staff, we would expect costs to be reduced by 5–10 per cent', or 'Based on our experience elsewhere, we would expect this programme to increase the department's performance by at least 5 per cent'. These statements do not guarantee that the results will be achieved; even so, some consultancies would prefer to use phrasing that is more non-committal. They may also have a disclaimer in their terms of business (see, for example, clause 10 of the sample terms of business shown in Appendix 2).

The plan

The items shown in the box labelled 'The plan' in Figure 5.1 can themselves be related in a hierarchy of objectives, thus:

- How are we going to implement this approach?
  — By carrying out this programme of work.

- How are we going to carry out this programme of work?
  — By utilising these resources.

The hierarchy can be ascended by asking the question 'Why?'

Resources may be drawn from both client and consultant. It is essential that the client recognises the resources they must provide, both in the conduct of the assignment and its management (see below). And, of course, the consultancy will be providing resources for a price; this price, with the other aspects relating to the commercial context of the business, will be embodied in the terms of business.

Deciding the method of approach

The approach to be used relies on an appraisal of how the consultancy team and client respectively are to contribute to the achievement of the assignment objectives. From this appraisal all the work on the assignment is predicated. As a consultant, you must be clear about what you are bringing to the party. The reasons why a consultancy is used are that:

- it has knowledge that the client does not have;

- although the client has the knowledge, they do not have as much experience in applying it as the firm does, or need the objective view of an outsider;

- although the client has the knowledge and experience, they do not have them sufficiently available to engage in the project.

Which of these reasons applies will determine your role, which has to be complementary to that of the client. At one extreme you can be highly interventionist and take much of the project on to your own shoulders. At the other extreme, the role of the consultant is facilitative, enabling the client to address the problem for themselves. Between these two extremes is a spectrum of consultancy roles, and you must decide which is appropriate.

Some projects are handed over to the consultant by the client and there is no further contact until the work is complete. Such assignments are often research-oriented. For example, a client might ask a consultant to identify the size of market and the buying criteria for a product in Zambia. The consultant would carry out the research and then report to the client. Even in a research-oriented assignment, however, a consultant will probably have some reviews with the client between beginning and end.

For the most part, however, assignments are cooperative efforts between consultant and client. For instance, in the ICC case study, the GM will probably arrange for John Smith to have access to records, people, equipment and so on, to enable him to diagnose the key issues (the level 2 intervention). John Smith will engage in data collection and report back with his conclusions. In the next phase, he will need to decide how the issues he has identified should be addressed. This may entail the active involvement of some of ICC's staff. They might, for example, engage in data collection, contribute their ideas, or plan operational improvements. Different modes of client and consultant working together can therefore be involved even in a simple assignment.

The next consideration in deciding the method of approach concerns the perception of the nature of the problem. A client may see the problems to be dealt with in more simple terms than the consultant, and would therefore not be in favour of an approach that treated it as complicated. In the example of ICC, the GM might see the problems of product cost as being entirely due to poor quality production. He may even have employed John Smith expressly to come up with the conclusion that high product costs are entirely the result of poor equipment performance, and to use this finding as a lever for getting capital investment out of his head office.

No consultant will retain the goodwill of a client by speaking against the client's favourite ideas on day one. Remember the dictum, 'Sell the client what they need in terms of what they want'; the consultant has to educate the client into the true nature of the issues that have to be addressed. The client's perception of these may therefore develop throughout the course of an assignment. This does not mean active opposition. If you set up an 'either/or' situation (either your view prevails, or mine) then you will lose – certainly in the long term. You should establish a 'both/and' view – ie 'We will investigate *both* your ideas *and* others, which from the evidence and our experience, we believe will help to achieve your objective.' The client can be brought round to the consultant's view later in the project.

A further point you must consider when deciding the method of approach occurs when a client is embarking on a project which represents a significant change to the business. You need to know whether the problem-solving processes available within the client's organisation are appropriate for dealing with this problem. For example, there are some organisations in which most of the transactions are oral and face-to-face – little is written down. One such was a business in which the founder and owner was a 'dealer' – an entrepreneur who had built the business on his skills in striking good deals. The method of problem-solving in the business derived from this process: problems were resolved at a round table discussion, culminating with a 'deal' – who was going to do what. While this approach was effective for many operational problems in the business, it was less effective in coping with more complex problems of a strategic nature. The consultant had to educate the client in other methods of problem-solving, setting up a working party to study the issues and helping the client to use a multistage approach to dealing with them.

In summary, therefore, in deciding the method of approach, the consultant has to consider these questions:

- What skills and resources can the consultant bring to solving this problem?

- What skills and resources can the client bring to solving this problem?

- What is the client's expectation of the consultant's role, and how appropriate is this?

- What is the client's view of the problem, and how does it differ from that of the consultant?

- What is the nature of the predominant problem-solving procedures within the client organisation, and how appropriate are these for dealing with the problem?

Other aspects of the plan

Once the method of approach has been established, the programme of work explains what is going to happen, and when. This is in effect the assignment plan. Sometimes clients find it difficult to visualise how the consultancy will accomplish the assignment objectives. The assignment plan helps by showing how the transition is to be made from the present situation to the new one. It is therefore a good way of building a client's confidence in the project. (Comments on project planning are included in Chapter 6.)

The programme of work will specify the tasks needed to be carried out by the consultant team, and hence the resources the consultancy has to provide. The fees that are charged to the client will be related to an estimate of the time required from each consultant, multiplied by his or her fee rate. The accuracy of the estimate of the time required is thus central to the profitability (or otherwise) of a consultancy project.

It is worth making explicit the resources you will need from a client to carry out an assignment. Sometimes these are clear – for example, when a member of client staff is to be assigned to the project team – but there are other workload implications for a client embarking on a consultancy assignment. For example, the client resources a consultant might need are accommodation, access to a telephone, use of secretarial support (eg for fixing meetings, typing, etc) and other office services. The consultant will also need time from the sponsor to carry out progress reviews. There may be more active involvement of client staff – responding to interviews and questionnaires, or communicating aspects of the project to staff within the organisation.

Changing terms of reference

It is not unusual for terms of reference to change during a project. This may be because circumstances have changed, or because new information has become available, which means that the scope or outputs of the assignment should change.

It is important that the same rigour of thinking goes into revised terms of reference as in the original. Again, it is essential that client and consultant have expectations in common. Consequently, it is sensible to secure the client's agreement and to document any changes. This is particularly important if the original terms of reference are written. Although changes might be agreed orally, a change of job incumbent or a deterioration in the client relationship may require there to be evidence of the agreed change.

TERMS OF BUSINESS

The consultancy is providing resources to the client and earning revenue by so doing. The fees and other commercial aspects of a consultancy assignment are covered by the terms of business. These will include:

- the basis on which fees and expenses (and any taxes, such as VAT) are to be charged, and how fees might be varied;

- terms of payment;

- other contractual terms, such as how the assignment may be terminated before its completion;

- conditions affecting the liability of the consultancy;

- expectations of what the client is to provide.

A consultancy practice may have standard terms of business that are included in each proposal, with variations, or optional clauses, which are tailored to a particular contract.

Some years ago, the Institute of Management Consultants (IMC) set out a standard form of terms of business. It is now no longer published, because the wide variety of consultancy engagements makes standardisation difficult. Nonetheless, it is set out in Appendix 2 to show the points that should be covered. It refers to the IMC's code of conduct, which is shown in Appendix 3. Not all management consultants are members of the IMC, but all should follow a code of professional ethics.

Companies that are frequent users of consultants may themselves use a standard form of consultancy contract. This will cover much the same ground as the terms of business of the consultancy practice, but orientated to the needs of the client rather than the consultancy. I have been subject to these from time to time, and the points of interest in one such are as follows:

- The client reserves the right to ask for replacement of a consultant if in *their* opinion the performance of the consultant is unsatisfactory.

- Consultants working on the project are subject to approval by the client, approval being based on the consultants' CVs and interview.

- The consultancy should keep records of all activities undertaken on the project, and make them available to the client if so requested.

- The consultancy can show appropriate levels of public liability and professional indemnity insurance.

- There are terms affecting intellectual property rights.

- There are clauses relating to non-solicitation (ie not poaching the client's employees) and working for the client's direct competitors for a period after the end of the contract.

These topics relate to all consultancy projects, and therefore can fairly be included as part of the contract. What the consultancy has to do in each case is to decide whether the terms are reasonable. Clients' purchasing departments are likely to have a standard form of contract that they will send to you for agreement. It is then up to you to negotiate with the purchasing department over the details of the clauses in the contract.

Determining fee rates

For the most part, the fees charged to a client will be related to the cost of the project, the cost being primarily that of the time spent on it by the consultants in the project team. (Other methods of generating revenue in a consultancy practice are dealt with in a later section.) The price charged to the client will be based on a fee rate; the level of fee rate required can be calculated as follows.

At the start of Chapter 3, John Smith's consultancy firm was assumed to consist of 25 consultants paid on average £40,000 pa. The fully absorbed on-costs and overheads were assumed to be as much again, resulting in total costs of £2m. pa. The fee level required to recover costs can be calculated thus: if average utilisation on fees (days on fees divided by paid days) is 60 per cent, the number of fee days in which this has to be recovered is:

$$= 60\% \text{ (utilisation)} \times 250 \text{ (days per year)}$$
$$\times 25 \text{ (no of consultants)}$$
$$= 3,750$$
$$\text{Break-even fee rate} = £2m/3,750$$
$$= £534 \text{ per day}$$

As the consultancy would also need to make a profit, the budgeted fee rate would need to exceed this, so a budgeted fee rate of, say, £600 per day might be set. This would have to be compared with market rates; if this fee rate is markedly greater, then it may mean that overhead costs have to be reduced, so that the fee rate can be cut.

Consultancies frequently charge different fee rates for different grades of consultant. These can be calculated based on individual salaries, as follows. Using the same example from above, the average annual fee income to be generated by a consultant is:

$$60\% \text{ (utilisation)} \times 250 \text{ (days per year)} \times £600 \text{ (fee rate)}$$
$$= £90,000 \text{ pa.}$$

The ratio of average fee income to average salary is £90,000/£40,000
$$= 2.25$$

(In practice, among medium and large-sized practices (with larger overheads) this ratio might be twice as much.) Someone earning £30,000 pa would therefore be expected to generate $(2.25 \times £30,000 \text{ pa} =)$ £67,500 revenue, and their fee rate would be set accordingly.

More usual, however, is to allocate consultants to grades according to their experience, skill and responsibilities, and to set a different fee rate for each grade. Table 5.3 shows an example of this.

Reductions in fee rate

There are circumstances when it may be appropriate to reduce fee rates, such as when a contract offers the opportunity to assign a team of consultants for a long period without interruption. Consultancy managers like large contracts, because:

- as a rule, the cost of selling is a smaller percentage of revenue;

- long assignments mean fewer gaps between assignments, when consultants might not be earning fees.

Both these points mean that the utilisation in a consultancy becomes potentially greater when large jobs are being done. Returning to the example of John Smith's consultancy, quoted earlier in this chapter: suppose the benefit of changing the sales mix so that most work consisted of long consultancy assignments, was to increase utilisation from 60 per cent to 65 per cent. The revenue would be increased thus:

$$\text{Revenue} = 65 \text{ per cent (utilisation)} \times 260 \text{ (days)} \times £600 \text{ (daily fee rate)}$$
$$\times 25 \text{ (number of consultants)}$$
$$= £2,535,000$$

Table 5.3 *Consultant grade and fee rate*

Consultant grade	Daily fee rate (£)
Director/partner	1,800
Principal	1,500
Manager	1,200
Senior	1,000
Operating consultant	700
Junior	400

This is an increase of about 8 per cent from that where utilisation is 60 per cent. A client, recognising these benefits of a long assignment, may use this as a negotiating ploy. In theory, the consultancy could drop its fee rate by 8 per cent (from £600 per day to £550 per day) and maintain its former revenue. In practice, of course, the decision is rarely arithmetically so precise. The decision to discount will depend on:

- how much you want the work;
- your relationship with the client;
- what's happening in the rest of the market;
- whether you believe you will lose the assignment if you don't discount.

During a recession, consultancies have been known to discount very heavily to get business. Apart from generating a contribution to fixed costs, the reasons for so doing include:

- wishing to get an opening with a new client, in the hope of identifying and selling extension work;
- wanting to keep the consultancy team engaged. Consultants need to be kept busy!

Expenses

There are other costs which will come under the heading of expenses, and for which the client will need to budget.

Value added tax (VAT) may need to be added to the bill. This is a matter of little contention when the client is subject to VAT, but will represent a real additional cost if the client cannot set it against the VAT on their own business outputs (as with government departments).

Bought in resources may be needed to carry out the assignment. These can include:

- specialist equipment;
- software;
- specialist advice or subcontractors;
- purchase of licences;
- and so on.

The need for these will depend on the nature of the assignment. On most assignments, however, travel, subsistence and accommodation expenses will be incurred. When an assignment entails travel to a number of locations, particularly if long distances and overnight accommodation are involved, these expenses can quickly mount up.

Consultancy practices usually have rules governing travel costs (mileage rate for cars, class of travel by train or plane, use of taxis and hired cars), accommodation (grade of hotel) and subsistence (eg a daily rate). These can provide the basis for estimating the likely expenses under this heading. For example, in the week that I write, I have just had to arrange a short interview programme with a client, which involves travel to locations in London, Bristol and Manchester, and we have agreed a budget as follows:

- London: no charge, as close to head office;
- Bristol: travel by car, at an agreed mileage rate;
- Manchester: travel to Heathrow by car; shuttle by air to Manchester; taxi to Manchester centre, and return.

Although this is a trivial example, estimates of expense on larger jobs will be built up in a similar way.

There may be other expenses, related to in-house costs, such as typing or printing. For the treatment of these, see below under 'non time-related charges' (p.120).

What do we tell the client?

Having estimated what the likely costs are on an assignment, what do you agree with the client? Again, the IMC has provided some helpful guidance.

There must be a clear understanding between client and consultant:

- as to the objective of the assignment;
- the fees or the basis of fees to be charged.

So besides defining appropriate terms of reference, a consultant's proposal should quote:

- a fixed fee, or

- a range within which the fee will fall, or,

- the fee rate(s) to be charged in terms of time (hour, day, week) or other defined basis, or,

- (recruitment work) a percentage of emoluments of appointee (with careful definition as necessary of 'emoluments'), any minimum fee or other conditions.

When significant expenses are likely to arise for the client's account some explanation or estimate should be given.

Some contracts are on a 'time and materials' basis: the consultancy keeps a record of the time spent on the assignment, and the related expenses, and charges the client accordingly. The consultant may give an indication of the likely total costs, but is not bound by that. The time and materials basis is used infrequently in consultancy *per se*; it still pertains, however, in other professions (eg among solicitors on domestic matters, or if the consultancy is providing a body shopping service).

Most proposals, therefore, are not on a time and materials basis, so you have to tell the client how much the total costs are likely to be to achieve the deliverables required. This estimate is expected to be reasonably binding – ie the client's expectation is that you will not charge more than the price stated without good cause. The reason for this is simple; most organisations have a budgeting system that requires budget holders to predict likely expenses. If a manager has authority to spend – say – £30,000 on a consultancy project, it can be politically embarrassing for him or her to feel obliged to ask for £10,000 more because the consultants had underestimated the cost of the assignment.

One way of avoiding this is to add a 'contingency' to your estimate – eg to tell the client to budget for 20 days fees' when you estimate the project will need only 17. This has the advantage that the client will either be charged less, or get more for his money, than expected. (Or, if you are cynical, the consultant will take longer to do the same job, or the consultancy will make more profit). But even if you add a contingency factor, there is the question, how much should it be? A small contingency will allow for minor errors or alterations to the assignment programme, but will not cover a large misjudgement of the amount of time required. Note that the purpose of a contingency is to cope with under-estimates of the amount of work required to carry out a particular project – not to cover changes in the terms of reference.

(Dealing with changed terms of reference is covered earlier in this chapter.)

For the consultancy, therefore, the question is one of managing risk. Furthermore, if there is keen price competition for winning an assignment, the consultancy has to balance the need to keep the price low, versus the risk of not allowing enough time to do the work.

This difficulty is compounded when dealing with multi-phase assignments. For example, in the ICC case study, John Smith is first going to diagnose the major issues leading to high product costs. The next phase will be to address those issues. Although John Smith can be precise about the amount of work involved in the first phase, that involved in the next will depend on what he finds out during his diagnosis. It is, therefore, difficult to estimate how much work would be involved in the second phase before the first is completed. Nonetheless, his client, the general manager, will probably want an estimate of the likely costs of the total project. Not unreasonably so; John Smith might ask for – say – £9000 to do the first stage of the work, but this is only the start of meeting the client's objective. The GM will want to know what the next stage is likely to cost. Is it going to be £10,000 or £100,000?

You are faced with a 'Catch 22' situation: you cannot start the work unless you provide an estimate for the whole project, and you cannot provide a precise estimate until you have started the project. There are two techniques that help to resolve this dilemma:

- Make explicit the assumptions on which your fee estimate is based. If, for example, you are carrying out data collection by interview, then list the locations at which you will be carrying out the interviews and how many people you expect to see at each. If the client then wants you to see more people, or visit other locations, this is a clear departure from the terms of reference, which invites an adjustment to the fee estimate.

  A similar approach can be used for estimating (as yet undefined) future phases of work. You could identify one or two likely scenarios that might emerge after the diagnostic phase, and indicate the consultancy costs that would be involved in dealing with these. Again, if you have made your assumptions explicit, findings that depart from these will provide the basis for amending the fee estimate.

- Quote a fee range. Unless you are undertaking a 'royal road' type assignment, the amount of time required to carry out an assignment is not totally predictable. Telling a client that an assignment will take 21 days implies a degree of precision that is usually spurious. If you say it will take (say) 20–22 days, this shows that at this stage it *is* difficult to be precise. As the assignment progresses, you can tell the client where in this range the outturn is expected to be.

Above all, with fees – as with all other aspects of the client relationship – the consultant should manage the clients' expectations. 'No surprises' is a good motto.

TERMS OF PAYMENT

The financial structure of a typical consultancy practice is such that although revenue is dependent on sales volume, costs are largely fixed. Costs arise mainly from employee costs and office overheads (premises, etc).

Such a financial structure means that cash flow has to be rigorously controlled. Take, for example, John Smith's practice, where a consultant costs an average of £80,000 pa with fully absorbed costs (see start of Chapter 3). Assume that John Smith starts work on 1 May on a three-month assignment, which is completed satisfactorily on 31 July. If he has worked 62 days at £600 per day in this period, the fees will be £37,200, against costs of £20,000 (being the cost related to three months of his time). The profit of £17,200 is healthy. The cash flow may not be, though. Suppose the consultancy submits an invoice for the fees on 15 August. The client may have a system that pays the invoice at the end of the month following that of submission. This invoice will then be paid on 30 September, and the consultancy receives the amount a few days later. The consultancy has therefore had to bear:

- the cost of an increasing amount of work in progress while the assignment was being carried out;
- the full cost of the assignment for two months while raising the invoice and waiting for it to be paid.

If this is replicated across the practice, there will need to be a large amount of working capital, which will add to the costs of the business. It is therefore important to keep work in progress and debtors low, and this starts with the terms of payment, included in the terms of business.

Because of the time lag in the example given above, consultancies like to have payment on account, or interim payments, made for an assignment. These will be against the fees agreed, but the fact that they are made before the end of the assignment will help improve cash flow. The aim is to quickly transfer 'work in progress' to 'debtors'.

In an ideal world a client would pay for an assignment on commissioning it. This would be marvellous for the consultancy's cash flow, but bad for the client's. Clients are (for the most part) also subject to the same cash flow considerations as the consultancy firm; from the client's point of view, their cash flow would be considerably enhanced by deferring payment until well after the completion of a consultancy project. There has to be a compromise. The client might make stage payments throughout an assignment, perhaps at significant milestones. For example, a recruitment consultant might be paid as follows:

- one-third of the fee at the start of the assignment;

- one-third on presentation of a shortlist of candidates;

- one-third on the position being filled.

Whenever there are interim payments, consultants should try to ensure that invoices coincide with the client receiving some value, as in the above example, or on submission of a report, or the completion of a phase of a project.

Fees might also be charged according to the time spent by consultants each month. In the example of John Smith above, the invoicing schedule would be shown as in Table 5.4.

Some practices on major projects might invoice more frequently – perhaps on a weekly basis. Whatever the basis of invoicing, this should be agreed with the client and summarised in the terms of business.

The other major factor affecting cash flow is the time lapse between the client receiving an invoice and paying it. Businesses often have payment systems that classify accounts payable into categories of payment at (say) 7 days, 30 days, 60 days, 90 days. Unless the consultancy insists otherwise, the client will put the account payable into the category that offers maximum credit, so the credit period should be agreed and specified in the terms of business.

Payment can be deferred if there is a query on an invoice. Businesses

Table 5.4 *Invoicing schedule – ICC case study*

Month	Days on fees	Amount invoiced (£)
May	19	11,400
June	21	12,600
July	22	13,200
Total	**62**	**37,200**

seeking to improve their cash flow may excuse non-payment because 'we have a query on the invoice' – whether or not there are valid grounds for query. Here the consultancy practice might agree with the client at the outset that queries must be raised within a given time after the invoice has been received, otherwise the invoice will be regarded as acceptable.

A consultancy's own procedures can also result in high levels of working capital being required. For example, in one practice, invoices for the month were raised by the 16th of the following month. These were then sent to account managers for onward transmission to their clients. Because of queries, account managers being out of the office, and this task being given a low priority compared with selling and operating, it often took as long as a further month before the invoices were sent out. This resulted in high levels of work in progress and debtors. The situation was resolved by the invoices being sent out without approval, direct from the accounts department to the client, but on an agreed basis for each assignment.

The final building block in keeping working capital requirements down is credit control. Consultancies should have a system for chasing up invoices due, but not yet paid.

Cancellation charges

A consultancy can incur expense if a project is cancelled or postponed by a client, particularly at short notice. For example, if a consultancy has reserved two consultants to run a three-day interview programme the next week, which the client then postpones, it is usually difficult to find fee-earning work at such short notice to fill their time. Even if the consultancy work is carried out at a later date, the six consultant-days will have been lost.

To accommodate these circumstances, a consultancy practice may seek redress by having a cancellation clause in the contract. This is particularly appropriate when running training courses, which tend to be for large continuous blocks of time. Obviously, whether the cancellation charge is levied will be subject to wider considerations of the client relationship. Part of the value of a cancellation or postponement clause, however, is that it can restrain clients from changing a programme needlessly – it becomes more worth while for them to put themselves out to avoid the cancellation charge!

OTHER METHODS OF GENERATING REVENUE IN CONSULTANCY

For the consultancy, the most significant element of terms of business will relate to the payments made by the client for the consultancy's services. For the most part, revenue is generated by fees, which are related to the time spent on a project. A perennial concern in a consultancy practice is the creation of non time-related income. The reason is simple: if all income is time-related, then once you have established your fee rate, there is a theoretical maximum level of revenue that you can get.

Suppose John Smith belongs to the consultancy quoted at the start of Chapter 3, which has the following budgets for the year:

Number of consultants   = 25
Average fee rate   = £600 per day
Average utilisation   = 60%

Assuming the number of paid days per year is 260, the number of fee days per consultant will be 156. The budgeted revenue for this small consultancy firm will therefore be:

Revenue   = 25 (consultants) × 156 (fee days) × £600 (daily fee rate)
            = £2,340,000

If the revenue is to be increased without taking on more employees, the options are:

- to increase the fee rate;

- to increase the utilisation.

My experience of fee rates is that price is rarely the major determinant in the choice of consultant. Other factors being equal, clients will choose the consultancy quoting the lowest fees; the consultancy firms quoting, however, will attempt to ensure that other factors are not equal, but seek to impress through their grasp of the client's problem, the quality of their people, etc (see the research quoted in Chapter 4). This leads to some tolerance of difference in fee rate; a client would rather pay £50,000 for a consultancy with whom he or she was keen to work than £45,000 where the assignment results are expected to be indifferent. So some increase in fee rate might be possible. There will be a market rate, and it may be possible to command a premium; even so, this is unlikely to be much above 10–20 per cent.

The alternative method of increasing revenue is to increase utilisation. Again, there is an upper limit to the number of fee days. Once time has been allowed for annual and statutory holidays – say 30 days pa – then the number of working days available is down to 230 per person. Out of this, time has to be allowed for:

- sales and marketing;

- product development;

- administration;

- training courses and conferences;

- sickness.

The time spent on each of these will be distributed unevenly across the practice; some consultants will do little other than operating on fees. Others may spend their time primarily on selling (see Table 6.2 in Chapter 6 for examples of the budgets for consultants with different roles). The point is that it is difficult to raise utilisation to an average of much more than 80 per cent without causing harm in the long term to the practice. Important tasks would be neglected. In practice, too, assignments do not fit neatly together – there are delays to their starting, which means that there is often waiting time for an individual consultant between assignments.

So the control of fee rate and utilisation offer only limited opportunities for increasing revenue. Consultancy managements usually ensure that there are tight controls on utilisation; it is monitored frequently (often weekly) and forecasted so that sales efforts can be adjusted accordingly. Fee rates are regularly reviewed, too, so the scope to increase utilisation and fee rate is limited in a well-managed practice. If the productivity of existing resources is optimised, how else can revenue be increased?

Payment of a retainer

A retainer represents but a small step towards non-time related fees. A simple arrangement is where a consultant reserves a number of days in a period for a client, in exchange for which the client will pay a retainer. If the client does not take the days, then the retainer is still payable. If the client wants more time than the contracted amount, this is subject to negotiation.

Suppose in the ICC case study (Chapter 1), the GM decides that he would like John Smith's services on average for one day per month – not to carry out a specific project, but to provide general advice and counsel. The GM might pay John Smith a retainer for a year of 12 days' fees. There would be rules about John Smith's availability – for example, it would not be in the spirit of the retainer for the GM to take nothing for the first 11 months and insist on 12 days in the twelfth. The rule might therefore be 'up to two days in any one month, and up to six days per quarter; a maximum of 12 days in any one year, additional days to be subject to negotiation'.

Retainers are attractive to a consultancy firm, as they represent a guaranteed fixed base workload. Their usefulness to clients, however, is restricted. Circumstances where they might be applied by clients are:

- With a technical specialist.

- To secure exclusive services (ie to prevent the client's direct competitors having access to the specialist).

- To secure consultancy services that are not project-based (eg where a consultant might be used in a temporary, part-time, executive role by a client).

A consultancy practice might also use retainers to secure the services of key subcontractors.

Decoupling price and cost

Professionals typically charge a standard fee rate, irrespective of the value of the work they do, but occasionally the fee can be related to the value of the work – for example:

- In mergers and acquisition work, a successful transaction is of considerable value to the parties involved. Professional advisers may relate their fees to the value of the transaction.

- In recruitment work, the fees may be related to the emoluments of the appointed candidate.

Sometimes fees will be success-related. For example, again in recruitment, at least part of the fee will be conditional on finding a suitable candidate to fill the vacancy. There have also been consultancies which, in their corporate development work, have accepted an equity stake in the company as part payment of their fees. In theory, consultancies might also receive payment based on the benefits that their assignment has produced. The arguments against this are:

- It can be difficult to produce a satisfactory base case.

- It may influence the consultants to produce recommendations biased towards optimising their fees rather than the client's business performance.

- Changes may not be the result of the consultancy project (eg reduced costs can result from a decrease in business activity instead of improved performance).

- Improvements may depend on the performance of client staff as well as the efficacy of the consultancy project.

- There may be a long wait for the consultancy to be paid, as the benefits accrue.

If these points can be satisfactorily addressed, the consultancy charge might be based on the share of the benefits. Some professional organisations of which consultants are members may prohibit this basis of fees, and so this should also be checked.

Using subcontractors

Subcontractors are paid usually only for the time they spend on fee-earning work. This generates a contribution, being the difference between their daily fee rate and the rate that the client is paying. The related overhead is usually small. Subcontracting has the further benefits that:

- it introduces some variability in the cost base. If the volume of sales decreases, you can reduce the amount of subcontracted work before you have to consider cutting staff;

- subcontractors can be used to bring skills that are not available elsewhere in the consultancy.

The disadvantages of subcontracting are that subcontractors:

- may not be available when you want them, being engaged on projects for other principals;

- are not subject to the same control as full-time employees. This may present difficulties in enforcing a uniformity of approach and standard of quality;

- yield less profit than full-time staff.

The indications are, however, that consultancies are moving the same way as their clients, in that they will use subcontractors increasingly in the future.

Non time-related charges

Consultants can generate income by charging for items related to an assignment, other than the time spent on it. Items that might be charged in such a way include:

- proprietary software;

- use of a proprietary methodology;

- use of psychometric tests and other survey instruments;

- reports (eg market research survey);

- organising conferences or training that the client attends.

For the most part, these represent income from the sale of intellectual property. The consultancy will have invested time and effort in creating the item (or may have bought a licence from someone who has done so) and is cashing in on this capital.

Sometimes a firm will make a standard charge of a percentage of the fee for 'administration, telephone calls, etc'. This will only approximate to the actual cost, but obviously involves less work than monitoring and costing every administrative expense. The basis of charging expenses should be clear to clients. The danger in making a standard charge is where it is part of the terms of business, which the client has not read properly, so that the first he or she learns about it is when it appears on an invoice from the consultancy. I have to confess to a personal dislike of this basis of charging for administrative and office expenses; I believe the fee rate should cover all routine costs, additional charges being made only for exceptional costs on an agreed basis. For example, a consultancy might charge for producing the material required to run a series of training courses.

SUBMITTING A PROPOSAL

Terms of reference set the content and terms of business set the commercial context for a consultancy project. These are usually brought together in a proposal, prepared by the consultancy.

Contents of a proposal

A proposal has a selling purpose. In summary, the functions of a proposal are:

- To persuade the client to undertake the project (or to endorse a decision already made).

- To set out how the consultancy would approach the assignment.

- To convince the client that the consultancy is well equipped to carry out the assignment, and that it should be chosen so to do.

- To lay out the terms on which the assignment is to be conducted.

The consultant's proposal therefore has to respond to these needs. The length, form and complexity of proposal documents will vary widely according to what is appropriate but, in varying degrees of detail, proposals will normally contain the items shown in Table 5.5. In addition there will probably be a statement of the benefits of proceeding. If the proposal is long, or complex, it may be helpful to the reader to put in a summary at the beginning to provide a bird's-eye view of the contents.

A proposal is a selling document, which should persuade the client to use your services in carrying out the project. Supporting evidence (covered in item 9 in Table 5.5) should be tailored to the assignment

Table 5.5 *Contents of a proposal*

1 An appraisal of the nature of the client's business, the background of the proposed assignment and the problems to be tackled.
2 Definition of the terms of reference and scope of the assignment with comments on the validity and any critical aspects of the terms of reference supplied by the client.
3 Proposed approach to the project describing the tasks to be accomplished and the methodology and techniques to be used.
4 A work plan indicating the timetable, sequence and duration of tasks and the total elapsed time needed to complete the assignment.
5 A statement of the expected results and outputs from the assignment.
6 Details of the form and frequency of reporting and arrangements for regular liaison with client staff.
7 Proposed staffing levels and the roles to be assigned to consulting staff and client counterpart staff and an estimate of the total time inputs proposed.
8 Fee and expenses quotation and invoicing procedures (which may be presented separately).
9 Supporting information on the consultancy's services, and relevant assignment experience and curricula vitae of the assignment team members.
10 Details of the consultancy's standard terms and conditions (or the terms and conditions applicable to the particular assignment).
11 Methods for assuring the quality of the assignment.

Source: Institute of Management Consultants

under consideration. The consultancy, therefore, must be able to access its assignment experience, particularly if the client wants to take up references. Whether dealing with assignment experience or that of the prospective members of the project team, it should be relevant to the assignment that is under consideration. Standard CVs for consulting team members are all right as source documents, but they should be tailored for each proposal to highlight the reason a consultant is particularly fitted for inclusion on an assignment team. A proposal should be a manifestation of the value that your consultancy practice can bring to the client. Clients are rarely impressed by statements of how wonderful the consultancy practice is.

Nowadays, organisations are rarely embarrassed by using consultants. Presentations made jointly by consultants and client staff at conferences are not unusual. Nonetheless, references to other clients should be made circumspectly when talking to prospective clients. Bear in mind that prospects will assume that you will discuss them and their business in the same way with your other clients. A client's permission should be sought before discussing with other clients the work you have done for them. From a prospect's view, however, it can be tremendously helpful to talk to an existing client – and a valuable selling aid to a consultancy, if given a glowing reference.

The reasons for using your firm should be included in almost every proposal. If the need for the assignment for which you are proposing is already widely accepted, then you may need to do no more; if, however, the sponsor or some of the sponsor's colleagues have yet to be convinced of the benefit of proceeding, then you should make clear the rationale underlying the assignment and the benefits of proceeding.

It is instructive to have a client's view of the requirements of a proposal. Table 5.6 contains the questions that Roger Bennett suggests should be asked of every proposal (taken from *Choosing and Using Management Consultants*, Bennett, 1990).

Resourcing the bid process

Bidding requires a finite time. For small assignments, the salesperson and/or prospective project manager may prepare the bid; for larger bids, more people may need to be involved. Because of the pressure to keep up fee-earning time, it can be difficult to get consultants to work on a bid in some consulting practices.

Table 5.6 *A client's view of the requirements of a proposal*

- Is the consultant addressing your specific needs?
- Has the consultant volunteered outline criteria for measuring his or her performance and for assessing the value of intended contributions?
- Has the consultant's intended work schedule been split up into clearly defined stages?
- Does the consultant specify the degree of risk attached to the success of the project?
- If sub-contracting is involved, how will the consultant monitor the quality of sub-contracted duties?
- Will the consultant be working only on your assignment throughout the duration of the project or will he or she be simultaneously involved in other projects? In the latter case, to what extent will collateral activities interfere with work done for your firm?
- Has the consultant considered the motivation and ability levels of your staff and the need to train them to implement recommended solutions?
- How much post-implementation help and advice is offered?
- Is the proposed timetable for the assignment realistic?
- Has the consultancy demonstrated that it possesses the resources and facilities to do the job?
- What proven experience of your particular industry and type of business does the consultant possess?
- Will the consultancy guarantee that the individuals with whom you negotiate the fee shall be the people who actually complete the assignment or will junior consultancy staff be involved? Larger consultancies often employ 'practice development officers' whose only function is to sell the consultancy to prospective clients. Such people put an attractive face on the consultancy, but may mislead you about the quality of its work. Always insist on meeting the staff who will execute the assignment prior to signing the contract.
- Has the consultant taken the trouble to identify selling points which distiniguish his or her services from those of other firms?
- Is the consultant willing to discuss previous non-confidential assignments of a type similar to that proposed for your firm?

But bidding is a project itself, and should be managed as such. The salesperson must make sure that he/she has the right resources to carry it out. This means in particular having consultants with the technical specialisms needed available to work on the bid. Ideally the bid team should form (the core of) the project team that is to undertake the assignment if it is won.

Bid approval

Even before *offering* to submit a proposal there should have been some form of qualification (see Chapter 3). The proposal does, however, represent a formal contractual commitment. Every proposal exposes a consultancy to commercial risk, and so there needs to be an approval procedure for all proposals, to assess the risk and to authorise the proposal.

The approval of a proposal before submission will depend on:

- who is authorised to submit a proposal. (This may be limited to named individuals, and there may be other limitations imposed by professional indemnity insurers);

- the risk involved.

Sources of risk arise mainly from the size and complexity of the project, which raise the following questions:

- How confident can you be of achieving the deliverables? If the project is going to break new ground (if only for the consultancy practice), there is a higher risk of failure.

- What is the risk of things going wrong? By definition, you cannot plan for the unforeseeable. What you can do, however, is look at the assumptions on which your forecasts have been made. If they are in error, what is the effect on the project? If the effect of any change of assumptions is to make the project more difficult, the planning has been too optimistic.

- What are the consequences of failure compared with the likelihood of success? Obviously you would not start the project if you thought it unlikely to succeed. If there are unusually heavy penalties for failure, however, you would wish to be more than usually confident of success.

- If you can resource the project, what would be the effect on other business? Would a very large project make you too dependent on a single client, and unable to service the rest of your customer base?

- What would be the effect of a delay in start up, or a cancellation of the project? Either will mean lost time while the project team waits for the project to start, or to be assigned to new projects.

There are commercial risks, too, independent of the size and complexity of the project. The greatest of these risks is not being paid. This may be because the client becomes insolvent, but there may be other circumstances, such as problems in transferring funds when dealing with overseas clients. Some (unscrupulous) clients may also wait until there is a sizeable amount of fees and work in progress outstanding, and then quibble about payment. This is a negotiating tactic aimed at either reducing the fees or getting the consultants to do more. Early in my career I was taught, 'never let the client have an unhealthy balance of the commercial initiative' – which they do if they owe you a lot of money. Happily, most clients are scrupulous in this respect. Tight credit control must be used to deal with those that are not.

Some consultancy practices have different (and more rigorous) procedures for identifying and approving consultancy assignments that are high risk. In any case, it is good practice to have someone other than the salesperson check over proposals before they are submitted. The motivation of a salesperson is to sell. An approval procedure at least introduces a measure of quality assurance, and at best can help to avoid a commercial disaster.

6
MANAGEMENT IN A CONSULTANCY PRACTICE

The person who can smile when things go wrong
Has thought of someone he can blame it on.

(Christmas cracker motto)

As with any other business, a management consultancy has to be managed and, if only in the long term, the quality of management will influence the performance of the business. It is not the purpose of this book to rehearse the general principles of management; it *is* useful, however, to consider features of management that are peculiar to the business of consultancy.

We therefore start by considering the roles that have to be performed in a consultancy practice. The management of the business is then analysed in terms of the need to optimise the value a practice adds to both its consultants and its clients. The remainder of this chapter is given over to considering the issues involved in managing the sales activity, and managing consultancy projects.

TASKS IN A CONSULTANCY PRACTICE

There are a variety of tasks in all management consultancies, which can be summarised as follows:

- practice management;

- account management (selling);

- bid management;

- project management;

- resource management;

- auditing;

- operating consultancy.

In a small practice, these tasks may be carried out by a single individual; in a large one, they may be spread among several people. It is not unusual for someone to be engaged in more than one role. For example, in the ICC case study (see Chapter 1) the management consultant, John Smith, could be operating as an account manager or as project manager in respect of this client. Subsequently he might conduct the project as the operating consultant.

An explanation of each of the above tasks is set out below.

Practice management

The task of practice management is to manage the business of the consultancy practice, or a part thereof. This is a general management role, with responsibility for producing a profit stream.

The survival and profitability of a consultancy's business are superordinate objectives. The practice manager therefore usually has the greatest seniority within a consultancy unit. At an operational level he or she will be setting priorities and targets and resolving questions of conflict between others in the consultancy unit – eg competition for resources. The practice manager therefore sets the (internal) commercial environment in which consultancy projects are conducted.

The practice manager will also be responsible for setting strategy for his or her unit, within that for the practice as a whole.

Account management

Or more colloquially, selling. As consultants derive much of their revenue from past clients, the task of account management is to maintain links with past and present clients, while also seeking new ones. Although an account manager may have a specialisation as a consultant, this may not be relevant to the client's current needs. Other consultants will therefore be engaged in projects for the account manager's clients. But when the project is complete, the project team will move on to other assignments for other clients, and the account manager will be left to maintain the client relationship.

Thus, while the practice manager sets the commercial context for the project from the firm's point of view, the account manager will be managing the context of the project from a client relationship point of view.

Bid management

A bid or proposal for a piece of consultancy work might simply involve a short letter. If the project is to be of any size, however, it will involve devoting some time and effort to preparing a proposal.

In some practices, this is formally recognised by the appointment of a bid manager. The task of the bid manager is to define the terms of reference for the project, to define the methodology, to assess the resources required to carry it out, and to prepare a costing of them. It may also involve assessing the risks associated with the project and, where these are felt to be substantial, seeking authority to proceed with putting in the bid. (See Chapter 5 for more on bidding.)

Usually the account manager or the project manager who is going to work on the project will be responsible for bid management. Occasionally, however, there may be people whose specialisation is preparing proposals on specific topics.

Project management

The job of a project manager is to meet the project objectives, within the allocated resources, while maintaining good relationships with client staff.

It is sensible on any operating consultancy project to appoint one person who is responsible for its delivery. The project manager may report to the account manager on project matters, in that the account manager is overseeing the ongoing relationship with the client and the commercial context of the project.

If there is only one consultant involved with the project, he or she has to take the role of project manager.

Resource management

It is unusual for consultants to be permanently allocated to a single account. The task of resource management is to deploy consultants among accounts and projects, and to ensure that their utilisation is optimised. Consultants might be allocated to groups for the purposes of resource management according to specialisation; in such cases resource managers may also act as 'product champions', with the aim of promoting their specialist services among the internal connectors – account managers – and thence to the consultancy's client base.

Auditing

The auditor is sometimes called a quality manager, quality assurance director, etc. The purpose of the task is to monitor projects against quality standards and to design and carry out procedures to ensure that suitable quality standards are established and maintained.

Over the last decade it has become clear that quality is not simply a policing function, but something that provides a real commercial and competitive advantage. The purpose of the auditor is to provide someone outside the sales and operating teams involved with the sale or delivery of a particular project, who can helpfully comment on how well these tasks are being carried out.

An auditor might carry out inspections of bids or projects to see that they conform with good practice. Inspections can be conducted after a bid is won or lost, at the conclusion of a project or some time after the end of a project. The auditor can also be a source of counsel and advice during the project.

This does not have to be a full-time role; for example, a consultant in Division A of a business can act as auditor for projects in Division B, and vice versa.

Operating consultancy

This is the default task and those individuals filling the previous five roles will probably also operate on assignments. It is common practice that even the most senior individual within a firm will do work with a client, although practice management and account management tasks may consume most of his or her time. Operating consultants may also have responsibilities for some sales aspects.

The mixture of roles in a consultancy practice

When you enter a consultancy practice, you normally do so as an operating consultant. The other roles and tasks above are taken on with increasing experience.

It is common nowadays for all professionals within a consultancy practice, however senior, to have a fee-earning responsibility. Most consultants will also have some sales responsibilities – see later in this chapter. What this means in practice is that there is a decoupling of rank and role – performance of a particular role does not imply seniority (except that of the practice manager). Thus, for example, A might supervise B on one activity, whereas on another, B might supervise A.

PRACTICE MANAGEMENT IN CONSULTANCY

I seem to remember from the days when I was taught corporate strategy, that the first question to ask when fashioning a strategy is, 'What business are we in?' Perhaps strategic thinking has moved on since then, but it is a good question to ask of a consultancy business.

Large consultancy practices have taken to adding a slogan to all their publicity material, which is the answer to this question. The slogan is usually to the effect, 'Helping our clients to become more successful'. But how is this to be done?

Consultancies add value to their clients through the medium of their consultants. Figure 6.1 shows a model of a consulting practice,

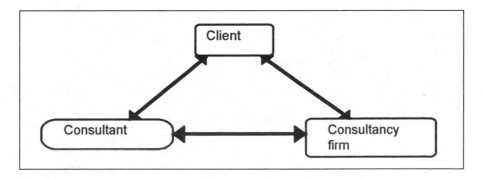

Figure 6.1 *Exchanges of value: model*

expressed as exchanges of value between consultancy firm, consultant and client.

This model is discussed at some length in Markham (1991), where the exchanges of value are defined. These are summarised in the Table 6.1.

For the purposes of business management, we need to consider the exchanges of value involving the consultancy firm, at both operational and strategic levels. The key question for any consultancy firm is, 'What do we as a firm add to the transaction between consultant and client?'

At its simplest, consultancy is simply body shopping; the consultancy practice introduces its clients to specialists who have the technical skills needed to carry out the work required. Consultants have the benefit of

Table 6.1 *Exchanges of value*

	From	*To:*	*Value*
1.	Consultancy firm	Individual consultant	Personal development, remuneration
2.	Individual consultant	Consultancy firm	Revenue generation, knowledge, access to markets (network)
3.	Consultancy firm	Client	Know-how, technology transfer
4.	Client	Consultancy firm	Revenue, corporate expertise and credibility, product development opportunities
5.	Individual consultant	Client	Specialist knowledge, past experience, know-how
6.	Client	Individual consultant	Sectoral experience, practice and enlargement of expertise, increased network

carrying their employer's franchise – they are being employed as consultants at least partly because they bear the imprimatur of their employer. The client has the reassurance of the reputation of the practice underwriting the work of the individual consultants. The practice makes a profit on the difference between what they charge the client and what they pay the consultant.

The thought will occur eventually to both client and consultant that it might be to the advantage of both to cut out the intermediary – the consultancy firm. A sole practitioner is the result of this thinking taken to its logical conclusion. There is none the less a role for a broker between clients and consultants, but this is more often the function of networks or associations than of a consultancy practice. So a consultancy firm has to offer something more in the long term. This can be considered based on items 1 and 3 in Table 6.1.

As shown in Table 6.1, the value that a consultant receives from a consultancy practice can be expressed in terms of personal development and remuneration. What a client gets from a practice is know-how (knowledge, skill and experience), the time of its consultants (in which they apply their know-how), and technology transfer – a permanent increase in the client's capability through working with consultants.

These are the factors through which a consultancy firm adds value to what otherwise is simply an engagement between an individual consultant and a client. The strategic task of the practice manager is therefore to optimise these factors, each of which is discussed in more detail below.

The value of the practice to the individual consultant

Personal development

Like other businesses, consultancies are faced with a 'make-or-buy' decision: do they recruit staff who already have the necessary skills, or do they develop their own?

Consultants wish to practise, maintain, refresh, and increase their technical skills. This they can achieve in part by working on consultancy assignments. They will also need to keep their technical skills up to date by attending appropriate courses and conferences, reading specialist literature, and so on. Besides technical skills, however, they need two other skills:

- how to deliver their skills in a client environment;

- how to effect change in organisations as a consultant.

Many people learn their technical skills as an employee and have learned how to discharge them as such. Working in a client environment as a consultant is different. Many topics covered in this book, for example, would be irrelevant to the specialist employee. The commercial environment in which the consultant works, the needs for marketing, selling and client care, the importance of project management – are all peculiarly relevant to a consultant.

A management consultant is also an agent of change. If consultants are to fulfil this role effectively, they must understand the pathology of organisations so that they can interact with them to achieve change.

There are, therefore, specific consultancy skills to be added to the specialist expertise of a new consultant. To a large extent, consultancy is a craft; skill has to develop through practical experience as much – if not more – than through formal training. Every consultancy business can therefore provide at least the practical part of the training component. Whether it provides formal training may be a function of size. The reasons for training consultants include:

- training may be needed to bring new staff to the standards of operating required;

- training may be needed to maintain and develop the skills of experienced consultants;

- new skills can be imparted and developed by training;

- offering structured approaches to personal development may help the practice to attract and retain good quality staff.

Given that consultancy is a craft skill, the apprenticeship model is a helpful one in developing skills on the job. Skilled consultants can supervise or act as mentors for those less experienced. In the early stages of a consultant's career, he or she may keep a log of activities in which they have been engaged. Their project work could then be selected to fill in gaps in experience, extending their skills, or improving in areas of weakness.

As intimated in item 6 in Table 6.1, the individual consultant gains much by working with the client. Personal development occurs not only through the development activities organised by the consultancy firm, but also through the consultant's assignment experience.

A benefit of working for a consultancy practice is that it enables you to work at the periphery of your expertise. Under the umbrella of the firm, you may work in a project team in which you can learn as much, if not more, than you contribute. Personal development is therefore helped at an operational level by assigning consultants to projects that help them to grow. This is something more difficult to do as a sole practitioner, where clients employ you in the centre of your expertise, and there is less scope for working in areas where you have little previous experience.

Remuneration

A consultancy firm will be 'branded' in the market-place, as an employer, by its policics on personal development and reward. It is important to manage the brand so that people of the right calibre are attracted as employees.

Consultancy practices are not exempt from the general rules governing remuneration – ie that the fairness of a consultant's remuneration package will be judged by:

- external comparisons (what they might earn if they performed a similar job elsewhere);

- internal comparisons (their remuneration in relation to that of others in the practice).

Where consultancy differs from many other employments is in the career patterns of employees. Often people who enter consultancy plan to spend only part of their careers within the profession – say four or five years – before moving on to further employment as an executive in businesses other than consultancy. There is thus a higher staff turnover rate at junior levels in a practice than at senior levels – the latter being populated primarily by those who have chosen to make their career in consultancy. This pattern of staff turnover has the advantages that:

- it enables new people with fresh ideas to be brought into the firm;

- those who leave will do so with (one hopes) a fund of goodwill towards their former employer, and will become clients in their new role.

What this means is that there are two classes of employee in a consultancy practice:

- those who are doing a job as a stepping stone to something else;

- those who see consultancy as a career.

Most people entering consultancy start in category 1; there is thus a transition point when they move into category 2. It is important that both the consultancy firm and the individual consultant share the same view as to which category the consultant is in. Misapprehensions on either side will result in disappointment. What some consultancy firms do, therefore, is to have career reviews with consultants at significant points in their careers (at intervals of three to five years). These reviews check the individual's career aspirations and potential and plan how they can be best met within the practice, or whether a move outside would be better.

The relevance of this to pay is that it points to two different pay policies for:

- those who will work with the practice for only four or five years;

- those who plan to make consultancy a career (and to whom the employer wishes to offer a career).

The pay package for the former should consist of primarily short-term elements – eg basic pay, profit-sharing bonus, company car. That for the latter should, in addition, have long-term elements, such as pension and stock options or another form of capital appreciation plan. This distinction is perhaps most recognisable in firms which are partnerships, where being made a partner of the firm is an indicator of being offered a long-term career.

At an operational level, pay is significant because it is (usually) the largest expense the firm has, and is a fixed expense. This can create problems:

- in cash flow – the firm has to pay the consultant before the client pays the firm;

- in volume sensitivity – if fee revenue goes down, the firm still has to pay the same salary bill.

Actions that can be taken to deal with these are as follows:

- Defer payment by paying salaries later in arrears. This will provide a (once-off) reduction in working capital requirements.

- Defer payment by paying a low monthly salary, but adding an annual supplement (a bonus) that brings it up to market rate.

- Relate the size of the bonus to business profitability. This will make salary a partially variable cost; when profits are low, bonus will be smaller, thereby reducing employee costs.

- Subcontract work. Payment to subcontractors can be deferred (which you cannot do with salary) and subcontractors can be laid off when sales fall.

Any action on pay must take into account market practice and the probable response of the consultants to the changes proposed.

The value of the practice to the client

Know-how and technology transfer

Know-how (knowledge, skill and experience) is the principal resource that the firm offers its clients. Technology transfer is the consultancy firm's ability to apply these to the benefit of its clients.

The reason an organisation might turn to a firm for help is for the resources that it offers. The firm may be employed because:

- it has knowledge that the organisation does not have;

- although the organisation has the knowledge, it does not have as much experience in applying it as the firm does, or needs the objective view of an outsider;

- although the organisation has the knowledge and experience, it does not have them sufficiently available to engage in the project.

A firm therefore needs to ensure that it has the resources (in terms of the skill mix and volume) required to meet the needs of organisations in its market-place. These needs are, of course, changing, and so a firm should aim to have the knowledge and experience required to meet these changing needs through selective recruitment and training.

Technology transfer relates to the ability of a firm to deliver its skills to the benefit of a client. Several points merit consideration:

- A firm should not operate only in responsive mode; it should alert its clients to opportunities and needs of which the clients may otherwise be unaware. To this end, a firm should continually be 'horizon-scanning'. Sometimes a large practice might have an advisory board or panel to help with this, made up partly of outsiders, such as academics, business people, politicians and civil servants. They would alert the firm to trends, opportunities and innovations, which might affect the firm's clientele and its own business. Even without an advisory panel, the consultancy business manager should make sure that horizon-scanning takes place regularly.

- The firm should be able to put together its knowledge and experience in ways that are attractive to its clients (this is product and market development – see Chapter 2). This does *not* mean that consultancy offerings are unilaterally the work of the consultancy firm; they may result from strategic alliances with other firms or individuals. Anyhow, they should be put forward as offering synergy between firm and client and, perhaps, developed jointly with the client. There has to be some basis for a discussion to start, however, and the firm should take the initiative on this.

- The firm must deliver its knowledge and experience to its clients effectively. This means that individual consultants can work in a client environment (see above under personal development). Collectively, the firm must offer:
  — operating methodologies that ease technology transfer;
  — the ability to put together teams of consultants who can work together effectively.

Overall, of course, the work done by a consultancy practice should be of an appropriate standard of quality.

Quality

Much thought has been given to the practices and procedures that consultancies must undertake to meet published UK (eg BS5750) and international (ISO 9000) quality assurance standards. These are embodied in helpful publications from the Institute of Management Consultants (see references). In this section, however, we look more at the quality of work than the procedural standards.

The challenge for consultancy – as for many service industries – is that, whereas the quantity and quality of inputs can be easily measured, those of the outputs are more difficult to measure. The inputs of a consultancy practice are the time of its consultants and their knowledge and experience. These inputs are allocated to projects, and are subject to strict control. The process of establishing terms of reference (see Chapter 5) is therefore crucial in defining the quality and quantity of outputs for a project.

Of course, an important measure of quality for a consultancy practice is, 'What do our clients think?' Intelligence gained from clients after a project, or after a successful or failed sales bid, will help to identify strengths and weaknesses of the firm, and cement relationships. This data must be collected carefully, too – probing beyond the superficial is necessary.

The task of auditing, which was defined earlier in this chapter, is central in quality control. The role of auditor is to bring an 'independent' view to a consultancy process – as far as an independent view can be offered by a colleague – and to see that performance, quality, regulatory and ethical standards are met. The auditor might also engage in the data collection from clients, referred to above.

SALES MANAGEMENT

How to manage selling becomes an issue for a practice with any more than a few professionals in it. There has to be some coordination through an organisation structure, systems and procedures.

We have already noted that in a management consultancy there are at least seven roles to be filled. These might all be filled by the same person who is a sole practitioner and (potentially) by different people in a large practice. It is in this latter case that problems of organising the sales function arise, because of the variety of people who might be in contact with a client on just a single project.

This problem is compounded when:

- there are several projects in which the firm is engaged with a single client;

- there are several buyers of the consultancy's services within the client organisation – eg different business divisions.

Should the firm attempt to coordinate all its engagements with the client through one of its own partners or directors? Alternatively, should it have different account managers to deal with the different parts of the business? Managers of consultancy practices have frequently agonised over the type of organisation that is best. I know of one firm that tinkered with its structure twice a year in an attempt to optimise its performance – without success; it is now out of business.

There are some general principles that can suggest the structure and processes that should be followed.

All consultants have some responsibility for selling

Everybody in a consultancy practice should recognise the importance of selling, and should be encouraged to take some responsibility for selling, even if it is limited to identifying sales opportunities.

Not all consultants have the desire or aptitude to sell

It necessarily follows that there has to be some distinction in roles and responsibilities. A practice may make the following distinctions:

- 'finders' (or 'hunters', referred to in Chapter 3);
- 'minders' (or 'farmers');
- 'grinders' (the project team).

The targets and expectations of how a consultant allocates his or her time might reflect this. Table 6.2 opposite gives an example of this.

In each case we assume that there are 200 days per annum to be allocated (the rest being given over to holiday, training, administration, product development, etc). The 200 days are invested in different ways according to the role of the consultant. A key figure to monitor is the conversion ratio – the 'return on investment' for time. The figures shown in Table 6.2 are illustrative only; each practice needs to work out what is realistic according to its experience. Qualitatively it is worth noting that:

- finders are expected to be more skilled at selling than the others;
- time spent in extension selling (selling to existing clients) should result in more sales than time spent on new sales;
- time allocated to fee earning is fully used as such. This means that selling will be fitted around fee earning for a grinder.

Table 6.2 *Annual targets*

		New sales	Extension sales	Fee-earning
Finder	Days allocated	120	40	40
	Days sold	600	400	40
	Conversion ratio	5	10	1
Minder	Days allocated	40	80	80
	Days sold	120	400	80
	Conversion ratio	3	5	1
Grinder	Days allocated	10	30	160
	Days sold	30	120	160
	Conversion ratio	3	4	1

All consultants engaged on projects should seek out and identify opportunities for further work for the consultancy practice

Opportunities can arise from a variety of sources, most often concerning an aspect of a client's business that is causing dissatisfaction. When such a possibility arises, the consultant should probe to find out what the real cause of concern is. Other points to consider are:

- does the client consider the problem important?

- does the client need external resources to resolve the problem?

A project team is well placed to identify extension opportunities; this topic should be on the agenda at each progress review meeting.

More generally, skill in identifying high-quality extension opportunities should be an aspect against which the performance of all consultants is assessed. They can help in supporting extension selling by:

- providing intelligence;

- providing introductions to key members of client staff.

Once an opportunity has been identified, you need to decide in what way it should be best exploited. All extension business must go through the same qualification and conversion procedures as new business. Although a particular consultant may have identified the opportunity, there may be others within the practice who are better able to convert the opportunity into a profitable sale.

Clients are a useful source of intelligence on your selling (and operating) performance

Consultancy firms nowadays often solicit feedback from prospects and clients on their performance, after a sales effort, or on the completion of a project. Follow-up after a sales effort should be irrespective of whether the effort resulted in success. As mentioned above, this is an important task for the auditor.

One head of a firm tells an interesting story concerning one of his fellow directors, who asked a prospect what had clinched the sale in favour of his own practice. The client replied, 'It's because your people looked more like a team than the competition.' The director probed to find out what had led the client to this conclusion. 'A very simple thing,' replied the client. 'When your competitors made their presentation two of their team gave a disparaging look concerning the third, who was presenting.' How frightening to think that a major sale was affected by such a simple piece of body language! But what helpful intelligence in managing sales training.

You have to be clear on the salesperson's contribution to the selling process

Only if you are clear on what you want the salesperson to contribute can you plan how to run the selling function. If the salesperson is simply a broker between the resources of the consultancy and the needs of clients, what is his or her particular contribution? Is it a knowledge of a business sector, or a network of contacts? Is it a capability in seeing the applications of – say – business process re-engineering to organisations, or access to particular skills in the firm? Or a combination of some or all of these?

I have come across all these attributes in varying amounts in consultancy salespeople in different practices. Each reorganisation emphasises a different aspect; this year we will be organised in market-related teams, whereas last year we belonged to mini-practices based on different functional specialisations. The danger of frequent change is that in the new organisation the salesperson's assets – networks, leads, sales initiatives, etc – built up over the previous period become devalued, and he or she has to start building afresh. Another difficulty is that the salesperson does not see his or her role in the same way as the firm's management. It is all very well to claim that the salesperson should be the facilitator of the sale, but sales people like to be heroes. They need their clear successes; facilitation does not provide this, so human nature will resist some types of organisational role.

Wittreich's rule number 3 (see Chapter 4) will always make it difficult to organise a consultancy sales force along the lines of those for a tangible product:

> *Buying the professional* – A professional service can only be purchased meaningfully from someone *who is capable of rendering the service*. Selling ability and personality by themselves are meaningless.

Much of the work in sales management in a firm, therefore, consists of resolving the tensions between specialist and selling activities.

PROJECT MANAGEMENT

Consultancy operations are embodied in projects carried out for clients. The effectiveness with which a project is executed will depend in large measure on the quality of project management. It is not the purpose of this text to provide a comprehensive treatise on project management; there are several standard methodologies available, some of which are used by consultancy practices. Whether or not you are using a standard project management system, however, from the point of view of managing the practice, you need to be assured that project management is being carried out to an appropriate standard of performance.

In this context, I propose to deal with the following core elements of project management:

1. Project planning — a forecast of activity.
2. Project control — monitoring actual activity against that planned and taking action to deal with deviations.
3. Dealing with the project context: managing the client relationship and dealing with changing circumstances as the project progresses.

There are other factors than these that affect the execution of projects – for example, the client's objectives in carrying it out, or the political circumstances in which it has to be performed. These topics are covered elsewhere in the book (see Chapters 5 and 8). In this section, therefore, we concentrate on the elements above.

Principles of project planning and control

I find the metaphor of a journey a useful one to gain an insight into the key components of a project.

In *planning* a journey, you have to know where you are going and when you need to be there. You must decide what route you are to take, which means that you need to know where you're starting from and whether there are any limitations on the potential routes. (For example, is the aim to take the fastest route, the prettiest route, or the most economical route? Do you need to make a detour to pick some people up on the way?) You will need to make sure that you have the right resources for your trip, (are you going by car or another form of transport? Will you need to take food?) and so on.

Suppose that you are to travel from London to Bristol by road, to arrive in Bristol at a specific time. If you are to be able to *control* the implementation of your plan, you need to monitor how you are doing; you need to have 'milestones', so that at predetermined points on your route – say, Reading and Swindon – you can judge whether you are ahead or behind schedule, and act appropriately. You will also need to be able to tell when you have arrived in Bristol.

On your journey you may have to change your plans because a road might be closed, or there is a severe traffic jam. Indeed, there may be a radio report that causes you to decide to change your destination – eg you are going to Bristol for a holiday, but reports of bad weather make you decide to go to Exeter instead. Plans may therefore need to change to take account of changed circumstances.

From the metaphor of a journey, you can infer the important features of project planning and control for a consultant:

1. You have to know the purpose of the assignment and why the client wants it done. The deliverables from the project and the timing of their delivery must be defined, stated and agreed.
2. You need to decide what steps are involved in achieving the assignment objectives, and what – if any – subsidiary objectives might affect this plan.
3. You need to ensure you have the resources required.

4. If you are to be able to control the project, you need to programme in some milestones – ie points during the project at which you can judge progress. It is too late to wait until the end to ask, 'Did we make it?'
5. No business stands still; during the course of an assignment of any duration a business will have moved on. It is, therefore, probable that the detailed requirements of the assignment will also change.

Other aspects of this metaphor are also helpful – for example, to go on a journey you have to leave your point of departure. Sometimes client staff don't want to leave the past behind, but there will be no progress unless they do.

Project planning

There is often a reluctance to plan, but planning is vital if projects are to be delivered on time, good client relationships are to be preserved and budgeted time and resources are not to be exceeded. One reason for this reluctance is that planning can be difficult in complex situations, or at the start of a project when there are a lot of unknowns. In such circumstances, it is sensible to break a project into a number of stages, each dependent on the findings of the former (see Chapters 1 and 7). The use of explicit planning assumptions can also be helpful in dealing with this. As the project progresses, the validity of these assumptions can be tested and the plan modified in the light of any revised assumptions.

Project planning should start during the bidding process for a project, when it will be necessary to estimate the time and other resources required to carry out the project. The elements of a project plan will consist of:

- a breakdown of the deliverables to be produced by the project, derived from the project objectives;

- a breakdown of the project into the tasks required to produce these deliverables;

- a logic diagram showing the sequence and dependencies of these tasks;

- the resources required for each task.

When the start date for the project has been confirmed, two other elements have to be added:

- a list of the actual individuals (from whatever source) who will work on the project, with exact details of their availability both in terms of the number of hours a week they will be working, and the dates when they will be unavailable;

- a timetable showing when each activity will be done, and who will do it.

If the project consists of a number of phases, a plan will need to be prepared for each phase.

In addition to other elements involved, every project plan should include:

1. *Milestones* at which the progress of a project can be assessed;
2. *Formal progress reviews* attended by the project manager, the account manager and the client. (Informal progress reviews may take place more frequently). These should at least coincide with milestones, and may be held more frequently.
3. *Schedule of deliverables:* when deliverables (eg reports) are to be produced for the client.
4. *Invoicing schedule:* when the client is to be invoiced for the project.

With projects of any complexity (involving a number of consultants), time should be allowed in the project plan for project administration (eg for briefing and review meetings with consultants).

If there are a number of people engaged in a project, a 'time and responsibilities schedule' should be issued on a regular basis showing:

- the tasks to be accomplished;

- who is responsible for each task;

- the resources (time, other) to be devoted to the task;

- when the task has to be completed.

A schedule may cover only those tasks in the immediate future; further schedules can be issued as a project progresses.

Project control

Project control is the process of monitoring actual activity and events against those projected in the project plan. It follows that if the plan is poor, control will be more difficult – control can be only as good as the plan itself.

The project manager should maintain records of:

- dates when tasks and phases have been completed;

- dates when deliverables have been made to the client;

- the consumption of time and fees and other resources against budget;

- any other aspects relating to the management of the quality of the project.

If a number of consultants are involved in a project, the project manager must gather this information regularly from each member of the project team.

It is often useful for the project manager (and consultants in the project team) to keep a 'project diary'   a notebook in which all information relating to the project can be kept. This includes notes of telephone calls, meetings, key decisions and so on. A project diary is particularly necessary when working on projects that are deemed risky. The commercial aspects of risk are dealt with in Chapter 5; there are also operating risks, which occur in the following situations:

- where the project is complex, or depends on innovative techniques;

- where a major section of the client staff is antagonistic to the project;

- where the client is unreliable – eg in not providing resources as promised;

- where the project is politically sensitive;

- where the consultancy resources are likely to be overstretched;

- where the terms of reference are ill-defined, or likely to change during the project.

The project manager should exercise control through *progress reviews*. These should be held at each milestone, or more frequently, as set out in the plan. Progress reviews should consider:

- progress: achievements to date and use of resources, compared with budget;

- problems, actual or anticipated;

- plans, including short-term action, addressing problems, rescheduling tasks.

This may be summarised in a progress report, which in addition might comment on:

- key meetings held with clients;

- opportunities for further work following on from the project. (See Chapter 4.)

The project manager should conclude the report with an overall appraisal of project progress and the state of the client relationship.

During the course of a project, circumstances change and more information becomes available, and so plans made at the start of a project may no longer be appropriate. Replanning should therefore be regarded as the rule, not the exception. Project plans should be amended accordingly. Replanning may influence two important factors:

- the scheduling of resources;

- the ability to honour commitments made to clients.

Managing expectations is an important component of maintaining a good client relationship (see Chapter 9). If replanning is necessary, consider what the impact of this will be on the client, and how they should best be kept informed.

Managing the project context

In this section we consider the project context and, in particular, three aspects which seem to cause difficulty on consultancy projects; they are:

- Ensuring that the client has the right organisational structure to conduct the project.

- Ensuring that the client is kept informed during the project.

- Responding to the need for change during a project.

Client organisation

All projects require some input from clients, if only to act as a reporting link. More is usually required – eg to take decisions. Not all clients are accustomed to using consultants and it may be necessary to advise a client on the appropriate organisation to manage the project internally.

Managerial and other resources required from a client should be made clear at a project's inception. The firm should also comment on the organisation structure that the client should establish for dealing with the project. The simplest structure applies when a consultant reports directly to the sponsor of the project. At the other extreme is a major project being run by an organisation, in which the consultancy firm is making a subcontractor's contribution within an established organisation structure.

Between these two extremes lies the project steering group. This can consist of the consultancy project manager and the client sponsor, plus other members. The selection of other members is significant. If senior members of departments affected by the project are coopted onto the steering committee, they should provide helpful counsel, and their participation should help to get better acceptance of any changes proposed. A steering committee gets a broader exposure for the firm, and reduces its vulnerability to reliance on a single sponsor. Obviously there are many variations on this theme – eg a project steering group that reports to a more senior committee, or subgroups that are responsible for particular aspects of the project.

Consultancy practices will have had more experience of dealing with consultancy projects than their clients, and therefore should always consider what is the most appropriate form of client organisation. In some circumstances this may mean challenging the project organisation that the client may already have in place.

Keeping the client informed

Client expectations have to be managed carefully, and this must be done through regular contacts with the client. Progress reviews with the client should form part of the project plan.

It is particularly important to make sure that the client is kept well informed during the early stages of a project. This is the period when the client may feel more insecure if nothing is heard; frequent reassurance that all is going to plan will build the confidence of the client. The policy with clients should be 'No surprises'.

It is a feature of consultancy projects that things occasionally go wrong, perhaps through unfortunate circumstances, accident, failure of a consultant or client, or simply because individuals do not get on. These situations can be managed and rectified only if they are recognised and acknowledged before they become crises. Very often the consultant can deal with them him- or herself; on other occasions more help may be required. This can be provided only if the consultant asks for help.

Similarly, client confidence is bolstered by achievements, and so these should be publicised to the client, whenever appropriate.

Changing needs of the client

When engaged in the detail of a project, it is easy to lose sight of the project objectives, let alone why the client commissioned it. The terms of reference should be referred to frequently, to ensure the project keeps on track.

Changing circumstances and new information may mean that the terms of reference for a project need to be changed. This is, in essence, a change of contract and in such circumstances:

1. The implications of the change on the existing project should be assessed.
2. The change and its implications should be discussed and agreed with the client.
3. The change should be documented, in particular noting changes in deliverables, timescales and fees.

No business stands still; during a project of any length it is probable that the client's business will have moved on. The need to change the terms of reference in such a project should therefore not be regarded as exceptional.

7

CONSULTANCY PROBLEM-SOLVING

Between the start of the assignment and the delivery of the outputs to the client lies the process of problem-solving. Problem-solving is at the heart of a consultant's job.

In Chapter 1 we saw that there were two types of problem that a consultant has to address. A problem that is well-defined and familiar can be tackled by reference to precedent – an approach we called the 'royal road'. By contrast, there are 'messy' problems, which cannot be solved by precedent. In both cases, considerable skill may be required to operate the given process in the client environment. In the latter case, however, a problem-solving process needs to be applied which is independent of the detailed nature of the problems.

In this chapter we consider an approach to problem-solving that can be used in addressing messy problems.

PREREQUISITES IN CONSULTANCY PROBLEM-SOLVING

It has sometimes been said that what a consultant does is to decide the answer to the client's problem on Day 2 of the project and spend the rest of the project proving that this is indeed the case. If it proves not to be the case, then he goes back again and chooses another answer and checks to see whether that is appropriate.

This type of approach may work with simple problems, but is of limited value when dealing with messy problems. It relies on the consultant's preconceptions, and allows little scope for creativity. By contrast, a consultancy problem-solving process for addressing messy problems must:

- recognise preconceptions;
- permit creativity.

Recognising preconceptions

It is inevitable that the parties to a consultancy project bring preconceptions that are fashioned by their assumptions. Your judgement about what is relevant in a given situation, for example, will be a function of the skills, knowledge and experience relating to your expertise and its application. Plainly, it is neither possible nor appropriate to try to eliminate expert judgement from consultancy projects. But when entering on any consultancy project – particularly one of any complexity – it is sensible to examine the preconceptions of both consultant and client to see whether they are valid.

For example, a firm of solicitors decided that it wanted to improve the quality of its client service. It therefore engaged consultants to design and run a training course for all staff, which emphasised the importance of good quality client service and suggested how it might be developed. In the event, the programme failed to improve the quality of client service, because of the different preconceptions of the consultants and the solicitors:

- Each had clear, but different, views of what constituted good client service.

- The consultancy had previously provided similar training elsewhere, so assumed that this would be an appropriate method with this firm of solicitors.

- The solicitors took the view that training would be sufficient alone. The consultants failed to challenge this. What was needed, in practice, was a framework in which people who had been trained could apply their training.

Whenever a client and consultant come together, each will have some preconceptions relating to the prospective project. In the example above, consultant and client had similar preconceptions; had these been challenged, a better development programme should have resulted.

In other cases, the preconceptions may be different. For example, a consultant may have an idealised view of how a business such as the client's should work, and will base his or her diagnosis on a comparison of what is going on with that of an ideal. By contrast, the client may see the work required of the consultant entirely in terms of alleviating symptoms.

There are dangers with both perspectives; these can be illustrated by an analogy with a visit to a doctor. Suppose you visit your GP because you have a stomach pain; here, the doctor is in the role of consultant, and you are the client. Taking an idealised view, the doctor might carry out an examination and say, 'I'm afraid you're a little overweight, and you have some skin blemishes. Your eyesight and hearing are not as good as they might be, and you look pretty unfit'. All this may be true, but none of it is about your stomach pain. Similarly, a consultant's diagnosis based on a comparison with an ideal will be unhelpful to a client.

On the other hand, you would not think much of a doctor who simply gave you tablets to take away the stomach pain, without bothering to examine you at all. The treatment may alleviate the symptoms, but not deal with the underlying problem. For similar reasons, a consultant should not confine his or her intervention to dealing only with the symptoms that a client reports. Of course, as with a visit to a doctor, a client will describe the symptoms at the outset, but these should provide simply the starting point for the consultancy assignment.

So it is inevitable that both client and consultant will have preconceptions about a problem when they start to work together. That they are preconceptions does not automatically invalidate them, however. A problem-solving process should:

- recognise that preconceptions exist and that they may have value;

- provide for them to be validated where necessary.

Creative thinking in consultancy

If there is a characteristic that distinguishes excellent consultants from the merely good, it is that of creativity. One consultant defines creativity as 'that which is obvious only in retrospect'. My own experience endorses this when working with a colleague or client, whose insight provides the key to finding the way forward in resolving a problem. Or, in my own work, having struggled with defining a way forward, stumbling on the key and reflecting, 'Why on earth didn't I think of that before – it seems so obvious (now!)'.

A good consultant provides his or her clients with insight, but you can do this only if you have insight yourself. Looking at problems in a different way can provide insights (eg what insights can we get if this problem is thought of as a water distribution system? a piece of music? a meal?). I do not propose to cover creative thinking techniques; there are plenty of books on this topic, and Simon Majaro's book is particularly to be recommended (Majaro, 1988). But it is worth while considering the barriers to creativity.

People are naturally creative but are often educated out of it. One has only to look at a group of children playing anywhere in the world to realise that creativity is an innate human characteristic. As an adult, to become more creative you must reduce the barriers to creativity. Roger von Oech in his book *A whack on the side of the head* (von Oech, 1990) identifies ten barriers to creative thinking. They are shown in Table 7.1.

All the rules shown in the table are appropriate at some time or another. For example, we may not be very enthusiastic to hear a surgeon describe the operation he is about to carry out on us as being outside his specialisation, or that he might be experimenting with a new technique that has a high risk of failure compared with other ones that he might use. Similarly, we do not want our bankers to be using our money in risky and creative ways if it means that we might lose it. Creativity, therefore, has to be applied appropriately. There is a time to be creative, using divergent thinking; there is a time to be analytical, evaluating the ideas created.

Table 7.1 *Barriers to creativity*

The right answer	That's not logical
Follow the rules	Be practical
Avoid ambiguity	To err is wrong
Play is frivolous	That is not my area
Don't be foolish	I am not creative

Typically, though, people working in groups mix creative and evaluative thinking. Someone will come up with an idea, which will then be evaluated by the whole group. (Sometimes evaluation consists in completely overlooking it!) The process that is being used is that of creating an idea and then evaluating it, repeating the process as required.

This process of cycling between creative thinking and then evaluative thinking inhibits creativity. Many of the 'barriers to creativity' quoted in Table 7.1 are quite appropriate when engaged in evaluative thinking. When engaging in mixed thinking, sometimes the barriers will be in place, some of the time they will be suspended. The problem for a participant in a problem-solving meeting is discerning whether the barriers are in place or suspended; the safe bet is to assume that they are in place, and so you should follow the precepts in the table. What therefore happens is that evaluative thinking takes over and few ideas are created.

A useful method of dealing with this difficulty is to separate the idea-creation process from that of selecting which ideas to pursue, and evaluating them into two explicit stages. First you generate lots of ideas, and then only after you have finished this stage, you pick out the ones that merit further investigation. The two processes are depicted in Figure 7.1.

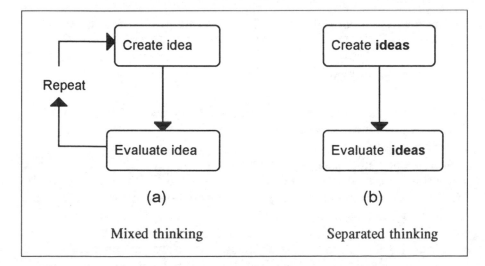

Figure 7.1 *Processes for dealing with ideas*

This latter process of separated thinking is used in brainstorming techniques. In brainstorming there is a creative period, where the aim is to create a large *quantity* of ideas. The focus is not on *quality*, because quality implies evaluation. Evaluation is suspended until a later analytical period.

A common feature of consultancy projects is that during the initial familiarisation you may come up with lots of ideas about the project and the context in which it is being conducted. The question, therefore, is how to accommodate this idea creation within a rigorous and economical approach to consultancy projects.

THE PROBLEM-SOLVING APPROACH

In the previous two sections we have concluded that an appropriate consultancy problem-solving process should:

- recognise that consultant and client come to a prospective consultancy project with preconceptions, some of which may need to be validated;

- include scope for creativity, particularly by separating the processes of idea creation and idea evaluation.

Set out below is a consultancy problem-solving process that meets these requirements.

Outline of the approach

The two requirements above can be met by using a method that has been used in science for many years, which is to start each phase of work by generating hypotheses.

At the start of a piece of consultancy work you have to ask, 'What can we assume to be true, and what do we need to find out about?' In what follows, I shall define a *premise* as an assumption that we can regard as valid – ie it does not need to be checked out. In contrast, I shall define a *hypothesis* as an assumption or supposition that is only conjectural – ie it needs to be checked out before we can accept it. A hypothesis is a contention; some people find it helpful to preface it like a debating topic with the words, 'This house believes . . .' A premise can be taken as read, but a hypothesis needs data collection to verify it. For example, take the statement, 'It is raining'; if it is a premise, you will take action on this assumption – eg you will take an umbrella if you go out. If it is a hypothesis ('This house believes it is raining') this implies that you are not sure whether it is indeed raining, and may wish to check before taking your umbrella.

The way in which preconceptions can be accommodated is by regarding them as hypotheses; similarly, all the ideas you have at the start of a project can provide fuel for hypotheses. Hypotheses provide a guide to data collection, which is directed towards checking them out. The problem-solving approach based on hypotheses is shown in Figure 7.2.

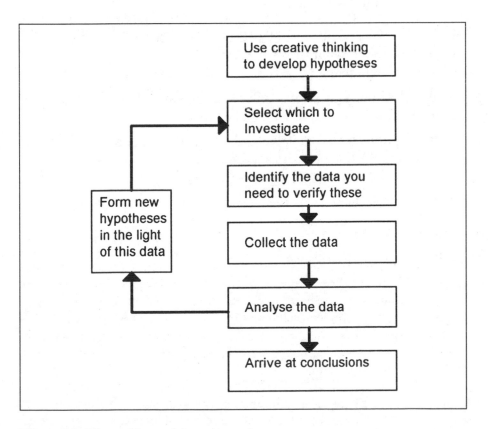

Figure 7.2 *The problem-solving approach*

The approach starts with hypotheses, which are generated by creative thinking. This creative stage is followed by an evaluative stage in which you select which hypotheses to investigate. Data collection is directed at verifying these selected hypotheses; during data collection you may also come up with further hypotheses. Finally, you arrive at conclusions. A conclusion can be thought of as a proven hypothesis; conversely, a hypothesis can be thought of as a provisional conclusion.

Before illustrating how this approach works in practice, let us see how it relates to the idea of 'levels of intervention' introduced in Chapter 1. These levels were summarised in Table 1.2 which is reproduced below as Table 7.2.

Chapter 1 also included some suggestions about how to decide at what level of intervention to start. In what follows, therefore, we will assume that you have decided this.

The first step in the technique is to develop hypotheses, but how should these vary according to the level of intervention? Table 7.3 shows the premises and hypotheses for each.

Points to note about Table 7.3:

• Hypotheses at a given level of intervention are related to the outputs for that level (see Table 5.2 in Chapter 5).

• The hypotheses for one level are premises for the next, hence each level should be dealt with as a separate phase (see Chapter 1).

• If your thinking is to be 'one degree of freedom more than that of the client' (see Chapter 1), then what you do is to treat the client's premises as hypotheses.

Table 7.2 *Levels of intervention*

1.	*Purposes*	The aims that the client has in mind when inviting consultancy help
2.	*Issues*	The problem areas that must be addressed if the purposes are to be achieved
3.	*Solutions*	What the solutions should be
4.	*Implementation*	The plans and activities for resolving the problem by means of the chosen solutions

Table 7.3 *Premisses and hypotheses for different levels of intervention*

Level of intervention	Premisses	Hypotheses
1.	There is scope to develop business performance	The purposes that might be sought to achieve this
2.	The purpose that is to be achieved	The issues that relate to the achievement of this purpose
3.	The issues that must be resolved	How they might be resolved
4.	The solutions that must be put in place	How the solutions might be best implemented

To illustrate the processes set out in Figures 7.2 and Table 7.3, we will again refer to the ICC case study set out in Chapter 1.

Assume that at the end of his visit, John Smith, the consultant, has decided to accept the GM's stated purpose of improving productivity, so there is no need for intervention at level 1. This purpose therefore forms the premiss at level 2, and so John Smith would start at this level by using creative thinking to develop hypotheses about the issues that relate to low productivity. He would derive these hypotheses from his observations during his visit, his knowledge and previous experience and his imagination.

My colleague, Anthony Macdonald Smith, has provided me with a useful definition of an issue: it can be prefaced with the phrase, 'I'm worried about'. At the end of his visit, therefore, John Smith might say, based on his observations:

I'm worried about:
       wastage and rework rates
       machine downtime
       operative waiting time
       customer expectations of quality
       overtime costs
       suppliers' prices.

Based on his previous experience, he might add other issues to this list – for example:

> I'm worried about:
> > the manning levels
> > work methods used
> > levels of stocks.

None of these last three points can be inferred directly from the account in Chapter 1; John Smith has added them because of his specialised knowledge. If you want to express the issues as hypotheses using the form, 'This house believes . . .', you can do so as follows:

> 'This house believes manning levels is an issue';
> 'This house believes work methods used are an issue';

and so on.

At this stage, these issues are only conjectural; John Smith does not know whether they are substantive or not. For example, by chance he may have arrived on the only day in five years that there has been a machine breakdown, and so machine downtime would not be a major cause of uncompetitive productivity.

John Smith may, of course, have created ideas that are not hypotheses about issues, but relate to other levels of intervention; for example, 'the GM is useless and should be fired.' This is a hypothesis about a solution, ie is appropriate for level 3, but not for level 2 at which John Smith is currently working. He can use it, though, to identify further issues by asking, 'To what issue would this solution relate?' This solution is about 'the quality of management', so he could add 'quality of management' as a further issue he might investigate.

Practical hints in defining hypotheses

- If you are working in a group in developing ideas, it is common to use a flip chart to record them. When they are coming thick and fast, it is difficult for whoever is writing them down to get down all the detail. In such circumstances, it is usual practice to abbreviate or to abstract the ideas. This is a dangerous practice. By abstraction or abbreviation, much of the richness of the ideas is lost, and where they are expressed imprecisely, it becomes very difficult to verify them (as we shall see when we come to looking at data collection).

- Sometimes the reverse is the case. When recording ideas during a creative session, those responsible for writing them down often behave as if ink was highly expensive! So write down all the ideas and then evaluate them; if the scribe acts as editor, it means that the evaluation is happening prematurely. Don't worry if you have some ideas that appear totally irrelevant during the initial trawl for them; they can be edited out later.

Hypotheses can be laid out diagramatically; these diagrams in various forms are called mind maps, spidergrams or cause and effect diagrams. This layout can often stimulate further thoughts and ideas.

This technique is applied to the case study in Figure 7.3, which shows the issues relating to the purpose of improving productivity at ICC. It shows the purpose (improve productivity) at the centre of the diagram. Around it are shown the issues that have been cited before, which have been grouped according to theme. Issues can appear in more than one place if that seems appropriate; for example, in the diagram, machine downtime appears twice: on the equipment theme, and on the systems theme, as a contributory cause of operative waiting time.

In practice, the best way of going about this is first to create an unstructured list of hypotheses by brainstorming and then to map them on to the cause and effect diagram as shown. Writing the ideas on the diagram will help to create more ideas about what others might be appropriate.

Hypothesis selection

Following up every hypothesis is neither practical nor necessary, so some process of hypothesis selection is required. This is where you have to exercise your judgement, based on your expertise.

The stages involved in selecting which hypotheses are to be pursued are as follows:

1. Disregard those hypotheses that are not relevant to the issues being studied. If the process of hypothesis creation has been dealt with properly, lots of ideas will have been recorded that have very little relevance to the scope of the project. By a process of inspection, disregard those that seem completely irrelevant. If in doubt, leave the ideas in.
2. Assess the remainder according to their relevance and probability.

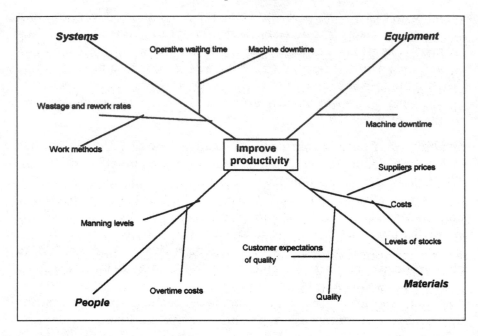

Figure 7.3 *Hypotheses about issues shown on a cause and effect diagram*

For example at ICC, salesmen's motivation may be an issue, but it does not appear immediately relevant to the purpose of increasing productivity. John Smith may also have hypothesised that, 'Competing manufacturers are engaged in sabotage'; this is improbable, so again it is one that would not be pursued as a matter of priority.

3. Hypotheses should be then classified into three categories:
    (a) Those which must be investigated because they are of central importance:
    (c) Those which could be investigated, but only if there were time.

    The missing category, (b), is for those that you are unsure whether to put into category (a) or (c).

After this process, you should have a shortlist of hypotheses that you are going to follow up through the process of data collection. It is a good idea at this point to take stock of your list of hypotheses; do they seem sufficient to you?

This is a sort of reality test; if you feel that having gone through this process you would still want to explore some items outside those hypotheses, it usually means that there is a hypothesis that you have not yet articulated. If you feel unhappy, therefore, think carefully through what you have done so far. Is anything missing from the logic? If so, what is it?

Defining what data is required

Data collection is a time-consuming element in any consultancy project, and so one of the most expensive. It is therefore essential that you are clear about what data you are aiming to collect and why you are doing so. It is very easy for the intellectually curious to go along some cul-de-sac and expensively collect data that has little relevance to the issues in hand. The process of data collection should therefore be directed to verifying the hypotheses that you have selected.

On this basis, you could produce a specification of what data is required, and then go out and collect it. In practice, consultancy requires more. One feature of first engaging with a new client or assignment is the process of familiarisation. The consultant has to get to know the client – the people, the culture, the business processes, etc – and the client has to learn how to accommodate the consultant and the project being undertaken. Each is progressing along a learning curve about the other, and it is unusual for familiarisation to be embodied in a formal process of data collection.

Early in the project, you need to develop a feel for the political environment in the client. Data collection therefore is open-ended, and you will be concerned with opinions as much as facts. Once you have established this feel, then your data collection can become more focused on the data you need to check out your selected hypotheses.

The data specification

When engaged in extensive data collection, you need to know:

- what data you need;
- what form it might take – eg what units it is measured in;
- where you might find it.

Specifying precisely what data you need becomes particularly important when working in teams of consultants; each member of the team must be clear what data he or she has to collect. For example, a multi-country study would be of little use if the information from each country was incompatible, because different consultants had interpreted what was required in different ways.

To illustrate the process of data specification, we will again consider the ICC case study, but at a level 3 intervention – ie one at which the issues have been confirmed and the work now consists of identifying how best they might be addressed.

Suppose that the issue John Smith is to investigate is that of overtime costs, and that he has selected hypotheses for the problems underlying this issue as follows:

- There is too much work for the labour force.

- People are not working hard enough.

- People are not sufficiently skilled.

- Work is poorly planned.

- Overtime pay rates are high.

Practice differs in consultancies in how they set out a data specification. Some consultancies identify what is called a 'key question' related to each hypothesis. This is a question which, if answered, would help you to judge whether the hypothesis is true.

The perfect question would simply be an inversion of the hypothesis: thus in Table 7.4, the hypothesis 'too much work for the labour force' would invite the key question 'Is there too much work for the labour force?' Indeed, some consultancies do not distinguish between hypotheses and key questions – confusingly, they call them all 'questions'. I prefer the split into hypotheses and key questions, as a key question can be phrased to illuminate one part of a hypothesis.

Key questions are particularly helpful if the hypothesis is expressed very generally and has to be focused before any work can be done in investigating whether it is true. This depends on the degree of abstraction of an idea. An example of increasing degrees of abstraction is as follows:

Table 7.4 *Key questions*

Issue: Overtime costs	
Hypotheses	*Key questions*
Too much work for labour force	Is labour force big enough to do work required?
People are not working hard enough	How do work rates compare with those achieved elsewhere?
People are not sufficiently skilled	What skills are required and does the workforce have them sufficiently?
Work is poorly planned	Is waiting time high?
Overtime pay rates are high	How do they compare with those paid by similar companies?

Spot is a small, playful, furry thing
Spot is a *puppy*
A puppy is a *pet*
A pet is an *animal*

'*Spot*' is a specific, concrete idea; 'animal' is far more general and abstract. A hypothesis about Spot will be more easy to verify than one about animals in general.

The 'key question' technique can therefore be used to help to reduce the degree of abstraction of a hypothesis. In the ICC case study, for example, you might come up with the hypothesis 'quality is poor'. This is abstract and difficult to verify, but could be made more concrete through key questions such as:

- Are wastage rates above the industry average?

- Do customers return goods as being of inadequate quality?

- Are quality standards set too high?

Once the key question has been phrased, a data specification can be prepared. A data specification defines:

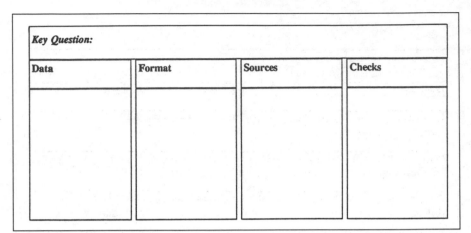

Figure 7.4 *Data specification*

- what data is required;
- what format it might be in;
- where it might be got.

The data specification is illustrated in Figure 7.4.

The figure also shows checks – where a particularly crucial piece of data is required, you may wish to have more than one source of it. Figure 7.5 shows a completed data specification for collecting information about ICC's overtime costs and how they compare with those elsewhere.

Compromise is often necessary

Data is expensive to collect, in terms of time, and thus in money. Often you have to determine what data is necessary and sufficient, and then you may have to compromise still further. The need for compromise is raised here, because hard data is sometimes difficult or impossible to collect. For example, it may be desirable to know the market prices of each supplier of widgets across the world, but official statistics may not cover this, and the manufacturers themselves could be reluctant to provide them to you. Alternatively you could be subject to disinformation. A compromise may be made by substituting qualitative for

Questions	Format	Sources	Checks
Hypothesis: Overtime pay rates are high			
Key Questions: How do ICC's overtime pay rates compare with those of similar companies?			
1. Current pay rates in ICC for overtime?	Hourly rates; basis of variation	Personnel department	
2. Current distribution of overtime earnings?	By grade, department job category	Personnel department	
3. Any local or industry agreements?	Terms of Agreement	Personnel department	
4. What local companies are comparable?	List of likely competitors for labour	Local Chamber of Commerce	ICC personnel department
5. What overtime rates are paid in these companies?	Same format as for ICC	Company personnel departments	Recruitment agencies

Figure 7.5 *Data specification*

quantitative data, and opinion or consensus in the absence of objective data.

The latter is particularly necessary with soft data – that relating, for example, to views and opinions. Soft data is important when dealing with matters of recommendation or implementation, when recognition of the political climate, and the culture and values of an organisation, may be essential in achieving acceptance. The more senior your client, the more likely he or she is to be concerned about soft issues and data, such as those concerning competitiveness, communication and morale.

Choosing a method of data collection

There are four generic methods of collecting data:

- face-to-face from other people;
- remotely from other people, by using questionnaires or similar documents;

- looking at documents and records;

- direct observation.

Each has its pros and cons, which are summarised in Table 7.5.

Quite apart from their intrinsic merits, when you have to choose a method for collecting the data you need, there are four other criteria to be met:

1. Is it sufficiently open-ended? Will it collect the data required on the hypotheses being explored? It is important that wrong assumptions are not built in (eg as in the question 'When did you stop beating your wife?').
2. Will it collect the 'soft data' required? This relates to people's opinions. These will be particularly important in considering the acceptability (or otherwise) of recommendations, for example. Hard data leads to technically correct solutions; soft data provides information on how to make them workable and acceptable.
3. What will its impact be? Remember that data collection is an intervention into an organisation. It has already been pointed out in this chapter that this, if poorly handled, can have dysfunctional effects. Contrariwise, the data collection method can be used to suggest processes of desirable change, or to give the project a suitable profile in the organisation.
4. Is it economical and effective?

Finally, remember that data collection is itself an intervention into the client's organisation. It is not possible for you to carry it out without in some way affecting the views of client's staff about you, your practice and the project you are undertaking. A well constructed and executed data collection plan can enhance your credibility, yield high-quality solutions and help to ensure more ready acceptance of your recommendations.

Interview skills

Much of the data will be collected using interviews. Your interview plan should reflect the type of data that you require to answer the key questions related to your hypotheses. Bear in mind that you could have objectives for the meeting other than data collection, such as:

- building relationships with the interviewee;

Table 7.5 *Pros and cons of different methods of data collection*

Method of data collection	Pros	Cons
Interviews one-to-one	Personal contact with the interviewee	Time-consuming
		Difficult to decide who to see
	Unstructured – you can follow up points of interest	Time-consuming to analyse
	The interviewee has made a clear contribution	
	Enables you to judge what sort of person the interviewee is	
Interviews one with a group	You can meet more people	Hard work – probably needs two people
	The project has a higher profile	Less opportunity for individuals to contribute
	You can collect a large number of views	People may be inhibited from contributing
Questionnaires	A well-designed questionnaire should be easy to analyse	Close ended; you get answers only to the questions you ask
	The respondent can fill in as and when he or she wants.	Must be self-explanatory
	Not time-consuming for client staff	Respondents may have reservations about committing their views to writing
		No sense of strength of feeling or relevance (although you can put in scales to test this)
		Low response rates
Document inspection	Good chance of getting unexpected data	Limited availability of documentation
	You can go at your own rate	Time-consuming for consultant
		Can be difficult to find the data wanted
Observation	First-hand information	Observation can affect the system being observed
	Good chance of picking up something unexpected	Time-consuming
		Difficult to analyse

- giving information;

- canvassing support for a particular view or opinion;

- problem-solving;

- decision-making.

Remember to leave sufficient time in the programme for data analysis as well as collection; for example, to write up or consolidate interview notes and to relate the data to your hypotheses. Interviewing requires sustained concentration and is tiring, so do not try to pack in too many interviews in too short a time. A good rule of thumb is to allocate twice as much time to an interview programme as the time you expect to spend face-to-face with interviewers. Try to structure data collection in a logical order so that key questions are answered first, and so that you avoid carrying out data collection which subsequently proves needless. Aim to get the data with the greatest 'leverage' first. For example, if the support of a managing director is crucial to the acceptance of your proposals, you need to find out if he or she has any strong dislikes or preferences fairly quickly, which could condition the hypotheses that you select to pursue.

Data analysis and conclusions

The data collection process accumulates facts which then have to be processed to produce conclusions. Ideally, what should happen is that the case for or against each hypothesis should have been made. A proven hypothesis is a conclusion, and so the conclusions from a full study would be a list of the hypotheses that had been proven.

Consultancy is more expedient than science and so, sadly, rarely as rigorous as this. The whole process is a little more messy. Nonetheless, it is essential that your conclusions stand up to examination. Like the layers of skin in an onion, peeling away the top layer of conclusions should show another layer as fine as the first; peeling the second layer away reveal a third, and so on. It is said of a former chief executive of an international firm that if you went to him with a proposal, he would take one part of your case, and ask, 'Why?' of it. He would then take an aspect of your answer, and ask 'Why?' of that. He would then ask 'Why?' of an aspect of your next answer. If you could answer these three layers of questions satisfactorily, he would accept that you had thought through your case.

Three layers of thinking can be thought of in data analysis:

- data – the facts you have collected;

- findings – an evaluation of these facts;

- conclusions – the diagnosis drawn from the evaluation.

The interventions that are required to address the areas of concern can then be specified according to the conclusions. Interventions are of varying kinds; frequently they consist of recommendations for the client's action, but they might also be action by the consultant, such as:

- training client staff;

- conducting a further project;

- taking an executive role;

- supporting the work of an individual or group;

and so on.

For example:

- It is raining (a piece of data).

- The weather is bad (finding). (This is evaluative, because the rain may not be bad for a farmer whose crops need rain.)

- We cannot go for a picnic (conclusion).

- We should eat lunch indoors (recommendation).

The reason why rainy weather was evaluated as bad is because there is an (unstated) requirement that the weather should not be raining if we are to go on a picnic.

Figure 7.6 shows the relationship:

- data lead to findings;

- findings draw you to conclusions;

- the specification of the intervention(s) is based on conclusions.

Each step leads to the next, by asking 'what do we make of this, in

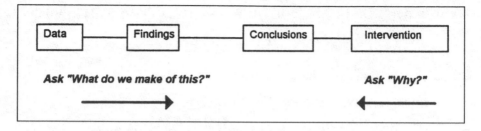

Figure 7.6 *From data to intervention*

respect of the topics we are examining?' Also, the logic can be tested in reverse by asking, 'what leads us to this view?'

Of course, in practice the process of splitting data, findings and conclusions under the headings shown can be a messy process. You can have difficulty sorting out what is a piece of data, a finding or a conclusion. A practical technique for dealing with this ambiguity is:

1. Divide a large piece of newsprint or flip-chart paper into three columns, headed 'Data', 'Findings', 'Conclusions'.
2. Write your data, findings and conclusions on 'Post-It' or similar type labels.
3. Stick them under the appropriate headings and inspect to see whether they are correctly allocated.

Use of these labels means that you can move a comment from one heading to another. A major criterion to use is that they all fit together. Once you are happy you have allocated your labels correctly, you should ask the following questions of your analysis:

1. Does the data lead logically to the findings and the findings to the conclusions? In particular, are there any alternative interpretations which could be made at any stage?
2. Are there key findings which have not been substantiated, which could be used to corroborate the conclusions?
3. Do the findings rest crucially on a narrow range of data? What would be the result if these data were inaccurate, and how inaccurate would they have to be before you changed your conclusions? How likely are they to be inaccurate? Thus the links between the various stages are tested.

There remains the final, and most important test, which is to refer back to the assignment objectives:

4. Will the interventions specified satisfactorily address the areas of concern put to us? Have we met our commitments to producing outputs? Will our conclusions form a sufficient basis to move the project ahead.

The assignment objectives should be held in mind throughout the project. It is easy to stray away from the original objectives and specify interventions which, although totally logical and valid, fail to meet the client's original concerns. Remember to re-read your original proposal regularly during the project.

CONSULTANCY PROBLEM-SOLVING IN PRACTICE

The relationship between assignment objectives and the problem-solving process

The problem-solving process links the areas of concern that the client has to the deliverables defined in the assignment objectives. This is shown diagramatically in Figure 7.7.

This follows the same pattern as Figure 7.2, in somewhat abbreviated form. In Chapter 5, we saw that scope and outputs were related in the assignment objectives. Figure 7.7 shows that there are other linkages throughout the process:

- deliverables relate to the areas of concern;

- conclusions are related to hypotheses (we have noted already that a hypothesis is a provisional conclusion);

- data collection links findings to the data required.

Also shown is the link between data collection and hypotheses; the information collected may prompt new or revised hypotheses.

Problem solving and the phased approach

In Chapter 1 we saw that the consultancy work at each level of

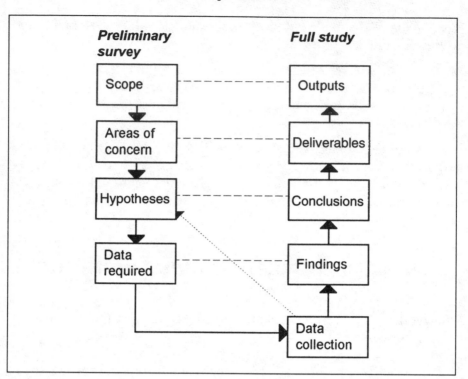

Figure 7.7 *Assignment objectives and the problem-solving process*

intervention should be treated as a separate phase. Figure 7.7 shows that each phase consists of two stages:

1. *A preliminary survey* The purpose of this is to select those hypotheses that merit detailed investigation.
2. *A full study* during which the hypotheses selected in the preliminary survey are investigated.

Besides these two stages, the first phase will be preceded by an initial appraisal, to identify the client's areas of concern and what level of intervention would be appropriate. If the project is then to continue with more than one phase, the subsequent phase would build on the outputs the preceding one.

Figure 7.8 illustrates the phased approach, showing the initial appraisal, the preliminary survey and full study.

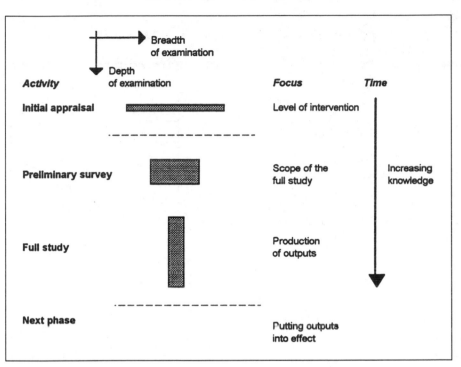

Figure 7.8 *Phased approach to problem-solving*

The diagram shows also that there is increasing knowledge as the project progresses. This means that examination can become more focused, with narrower breadth and greater depth at each stage.

The initial appraisal may vary in depth from a short conversation to more extensive work, although it would *not* be substantial. If a substantial piece of work is needed, it usually means that the project has to start at a level 1 intervention. The preliminary survey can be a substantial piece of work, more focused and in greater depth than the initial appraisal.

The full study is in turn still more focused and in greater depth than the preliminary survey. It may be broken down into steps, as with any project. On completion of the full study, the project may then move on to the next phase of work.

8

INTERVENTION

It is now more than 60 years since the celebrated Hawthorne experiments were carried out. Although they are well known, it is worth recapping on the main features.

At the turn of the century, Frederick Winslow Taylor had shown how productivity in factories could be vastly increased by work study and the application of incentives. Subsequently the era of 'scientific management' resulted in his techniques – and those of other early management consultants – being applied across industry. The study of how to improve productivity became widespread.

One such study, led by Elton Mayo, concerned the effect of illumination on productivity. His team conducted their research at the Hawthorne works of the Western Electric Company, just outside Chicago. The experimental method consisted of taking a small group of workers, who were assembling relays, and getting them to carry out their work in a separate room away from the main factory floor, where the illumination could be varied.

During the study, productivity increased. What was confusing, however, was that this was unrelated to the level of the illumination. The researchers eventually ascribed this effect to the fact that the work group was responding to the interest of the researchers themselves. Since then, the 'Hawthorne effect' has been used to describe the fact that an observer might have an effect on the work of a group that he or she is observing.

The Hawthorne experiments also marked a turning point in the way that organisations were popularly conceived. Scientific management achieved increases in productivity by considering people as units of production. Following on from the Hawthorne experiments, the 'human relations' school of thought showed that further increases in productivity could be achieved if people were treated as people.

The relevance of the Hawthorne experiments to consultants is twofold:

- The actions that a consultant takes on an assignment are rarely without effect on the client system. For example, data gathering is not a passive activity; asking a particular question may create a train of thought in the interviewee that changes the way they look at the world and the decisions they take.

- Consultancy is not just about problem-solving – it is about helping clients perform better, which means dealing with the human as well as the technical aspects.

Much has been written on this subject; for a detailed study, see Schein's books on *Process Consultation* (Schein, 1988). In this chapter, however, I will focus on the intervention stage of the consultant's interaction with the client, particularly in respect of getting recommendations accepted. By 'recommendations' I mean not only substantive advice from the consultant as an expert, but also suggestions about processes in which a client might engage, with the consultant in the role of facilitator.

Getting acceptance of a consultant's recommendations is often accomplished in two stages:

- the translation of recommendations into decisions, which is done at an executive level in an organisation;

- the translation of recommendations (or decisions) into action, which may be done at more junior levels.

Intervention is discussed in these two respects in this chapter; but first, we need to consider how to formulate high-quality recommendations.

FORMULATING HIGH-QUALITY RECOMMENDATIONS

Consultants are sometimes likened to giant birds that fly into an organisation, excrete a fat report, and then fly off again. Obviously there will be occasions when this is just what is wanted. But if the intention is to do something more, failure may be the result of poor recommendations.

So, what makes for high-quality recommendations? Three criteria should be considered:

- *Technical adequacy*   Will they work?
- *Acceptability* to the client.
- *Doability*   The capacity of the client to implement them.

Technical adequacy

This criterion is the most familiar and straightforward; will the recommendations help the client to address the assignment objectives satisfactorily? Given that the purpose of a consultancy assignment is to do just this, then I hope that the answer is 'Yes'. If in doubt, refer to the terms of reference!

Every assignment should also have a spice of originality to its recommendations. No two clients are identical, and so it is unlikely that identical recommendations will be suitable. If they are, it should be because alternatives have been considered and abandoned.

Acceptability

Much of this chapter is devoted to helping the consultant get his or her recommendations accepted by a client. But if a recommendation is profoundly unacceptable – ie not in the interests of the client or of influential members of client staff – then compromise is necessary. For example, a consultancy team advising on organisational issues took the view that the newly appointed chief executive was the wrong person to lead a particular client forward. The ideal recommendation was to replace him, but soundings showed there was insufficient support for this option among the other directors. The compromise was to strengthen the executive team so that the chief executive would have adequate support in carrying out the tasks in the areas in which he was weakest.

Acceptability will also be conditional on the culture and values of the organisation. For instance, there may be rules about how change may be introduced – eg no redundancies.

Doability

The history of foreign aid to less developed countries abounds in stories of well-meaning donations of advanced equipment that cannot be repaired when it breaks down, because of a lack of spare parts, or the absence of an infrastructure to distribute them, or insufficient skill to fit them properly. From this difficulty arose the notion of intermediate technology – not the most advanced, but that which a recipient country can sustain.

Similar considerations apply to clients; their organisations may be unable to sustain the 'best' technical solution. The consultant may install it, and it will work well for a while, but at the first sign of difficulty the new system breaks down irretrievably as far as the client is concerned. So again, compromise may be necessary. Points for consideration are:

1. Has the client got the necessary resources (managerial, financial, etc) to sustain this solution?
2. Has the client got the skills (technical, systems, etc) to support this solution?
3. Is the solution consistent with the client's culture and style of management? Solutions that require a fundamental change in client culture or behaviour are more susceptible to failure.

TRANSLATING RECOMMENDATIONS INTO DECISIONS

Only if recommendations are accepted by executives will they be translated into decisions. Whether they are accepted depends on two factors:

- the consultant's influence, which will affect the weight that the client attaches to what the consultant says;

- the attractiveness (or otherwise) of the specific recommendations.

If a consultant's view carries little weight, then it will be difficult for him or her to get recommendations accepted, irrespective of how sound they are.

This consideration is not only about how to present recommendations to best effect. Recommendations are like tender young plants; the ground has to be prepared carefully beforehand if they are to flourish. Similarly, the conduct of the assignment must provide a basis for the warm reception of the recommendations.

The nature of a consultant's influence

First, therefore, let us consider the nature of a consultant's influence.

By definition, a consultant has no legitimate executive authority within the client organisation. Sometimes a consultant may be delegated authority – eg members of the client's staff may be assigned to work under his or her direction on a consultancy project – but this authority will be within strict confines. For the most part, a consultant can only influence the decision-making processes within a client.

So what power does the consultant have? It is the consultant's expertise – knowledge, skill, experience, know-how – that gets him or her admission into a client organisation. If you do not have expertise, then you cannot act as an expert. Once inside an organisation, another type of power also comes into play – connection power. The consultant will often have been appointed by executives more senior than the client staff with whom the consultant is working on a day-to-day basis. Connection power gives a power of sanction – if junior staff are not cooperative, then the consultant can use his or her connections at a senior level to make things happen. Because of the connection with key people, the consultant may come into possession of information about situations, plans and so on, which is not generally known. This can help in exerting influence. Moreover, client staff may pay more heed to the consultant if they believe that he or she is privy to – and has an influence over – their future careers.

It is the perception of power that leads to influence – for example, irrespective of how skilled you are, if you are not credited with any expertise, you will have no expert power. You therefore need to make careful efforts to develop your influence by:

- using your expertise for cultivating connections within the client;

- using these connections to exercise influence.

Your behaviour will also determine the degree of influence you have. Consider:

1. *How do you see yourself?* People will initially take you at your own

valuation. If you have a low opinion of yourself, your abilities, or your standing with the client, this will come across. Consultants should not be arrogant, but neither are they supplicants.

2. *What impression do you make?* From day one of their career, consultants are taught that first impressions count. It is a point so well known that it may not seem worth while repeating, yet it still creates difficulties. So remember that your appearance, what you say, and how you comport yourself, will affect the impression that you make. And be natural – clients are offended if you try to pretend to be something that you're not.

3. *How do you and your colleagues treat one another?* If you treat one another with disdain, what is the client to make of this? For example, there was a director of a consultancy who was introducing a young consultant to a client. During the meeting, the director peremptorily asked his colleague to fetch his briefcase from his car. Although the director was undoubtedly the senior, he had undermined the standing of his junior colleague with that client from the start.

Optimising expert power

For the most part, a consultant starts with a fund of expert power – an expectation that he or she is expert in their area of specialisation. What the consultant says or does enhances or diminishes this. The wrong appearance, asking foolish questions, revealing a lack of knowledge and so on will undermine the perception of the consultant's expertise.

The perception of expert power will derive not only from what the consultant says and does, but also from:

- the label of 'consultant';

- the 'franchise' of the consultant's firm.

Being labelled a consultant is not always a passport to friendly acceptance by client staff. Negative feelings can arise from:

- consultancy projects in the past that have led to painful change;

- previous experience of poor quality consultancy service;

- dislike of the consultant's role, fee rate etc.

Nevertheless, the label of consultant should create an expectation of having at least some expertise. The 'franchise' of the consultancy firm derives from its reputation. If the consultant works for a practice that is known to the client, he or she will take on some of the attributes of that consultancy. (By analogy, if you go as a patient into a hospital, you assume that the person called 'doctor' knows about medicine!)

Developing expert power comes by displaying technical expertise. This must be complemented by understanding. Airing technical knowledge is unlikely to impress a client; applying technical knowledge to a client's problems in a helpful way, and explaining this in terms the client understands, will help to enhance your influence.

Optimising connection power

Connection power derives from contact with important or influential members of the client's staff, so it is important therefore that a consultant preserves connections with them. For example, the mechanism of a steering committee can be used in project management to maintain contacts with senior people, and to escalate the level of contact within an organisation.

Maintaining appropriate contacts within the client organisation is, in effect, networking – a concept that we have already come across in connection with selling. In this instance the consultant is trying to 'sell' him or herself within the client organisation. To this end, therefore, you should seek to establish and maintain a variety of links among client staff. Every interaction with the client will affect how you are perceived. While preparing for meetings, interviews, presentations or any other interaction, therefore, you must consider not only the business of the meeting, but also how it might be used to develop your influence in the client.

For example, suppose that at the start of an assignment you have to collect information from each director on the client's board. This provides an excellent opportunity for the consultant to form relationships with the key executives in the client organisation. The risk is that the consultant sees this solely as data collection, thereby missing this opportunity.

In deciding with whom to network, the concept of the 'dominant coalition' is helpful. In his book *Organisation Dynamics* (Kotter, 1978), Kotter defines the dominant coalition as 'the ... minimum group of co-operating employees who oversee the organisation as a whole and control its basic policy making.' This definition could equally well be applied to a part of an organisation. The key points worth noting relevant to consultants' influence are:

- The dominant coalition does not necessarily coincide with the most senior management group in (that part of) the organisation.

- It is not only who they are, but their objectives and strategies that are important.

- The relationships among the members are also important.

The messages for consultants are therefore:

- Beware those who do not have high rank, but are nonetheless influential, as well as those who have high-sounding rank but little influence.

- Be aware of the objectives and strategies of the dominant coalition as setting the context for decisions and actions they might take. When dealing with parts of an organisation, recognise that these objectives and strategies will actively involve the relationships with the other parts of the organisation.

- Where the dominant coalition is not united, more work will be required to secure acceptance of recommendations than if it is united.

Exercising influence

So far we have been considering the nature of a consultant's influence – the accretion of expert and connection power, so that when he or she speaks, what is said commands at least some attention.

Next, we need to consider the exercise of this influence, so as to get acceptance of particular recommendations. Getting acceptance of recommendations starts long before their presentation, and entails managing informal as well as formal communications with the client.

Informal communications

As mentioned above, all interactions with a client are interventions into the client environment, and have to be managed as such. For example, in an interview programme, the consultant might start the process of change by asking a single question – eg 'Has the company ever considered moving to a lower cost location?' might prompt this consideration if none had previously been given.

It is often useful to get a reaction to ideas well before presenting them, during progress reviews and other meetings or encounters with key members of the dominant coalition. You can trail them without commitment – eg 'One of the suggestions that has been made is ...', or, 'We came across this idea at another client's ...'. Discussing the way your thinking is going can also elicit useful information that can help you in reformulating or refining recommendations.

Formal communications

Formal communications will consist of face-to-face presentations and meetings, and reports and other written communications. This book does not cover the details of how to prepare and deliver presentations to a high standard (see Markham, 1991 for details on these).

The choice of whom to communicate to is important. Members of the dominant coalition are an obvious choice, but remember:

- You may not have direct access to members of the dominant coalition; you may therefore need to deal (at least initially) with connectors who act as gatekeepers to them.

- The power to say 'No' is widely distributed throughout an organisation. Although someone may not be able to make something happen, they may be able to stop it. So remember you will need to convince those who can stop a proposal, as well as those who can make it happen.

Matching communication style with the decision-making style of the organisation

Choosing an appropriate style of communication is also important. The style with which an organisation takes decisions is on a spectrum from action-oriented to reflective. Organisations with an *action-oriented style* will like face-to-face communications. They will appreciate being presented with the key points and will aim to sort out what has to be done at a single meeting. By contrast, those organisations with a *reflective* style will prefer to receive a paper on a topic, which is then discussed at a committee meeting.

Working with each style has its pros and cons. The action-oriented likes to get things done quickly. The disadvantage is that this does not work when dealing with complex problems. For example, one professional services firm was reviewing how it could best develop its business in the midst of a recession. The approach among partners was for each to assert what the solution was and to seek to persuade their colleagues of it. This did not allow any effort to be put into thinking about what the nature of the problem was, and so the action taken was not particularly effective.

The reflective style does allow debate about the nature of the problem, but it can also be frustrating for an action-oriented organisation. For example, a financial services group was considering restructuring its bonus plan, which had profound implications for their (very strong) culture. The consultant sought to explore the issues by presenting a series of papers to a steering committee. The steering committee wanted more speedy action, and so became increasingly frustrated, until the work reached the implementation stage. Here, the consultant had failed to match the required style; a more action-oriented approach was required.

This difference of style applies to individuals, too, who can be action-oriented, or reflective, or somewhere between the two. The consultant needs to suit the manner of communication to the style. Papers may be read only cursorily by the action-oriented, while a reflective manager will not like to make a decision of any moment without a paper being presented on the topic first.

One of a consultant's functions is educative – so that they leave clients better able to deal with the matters of concern addressed on the assignment (see 'Transfer' later in this chapter). The consultant may need to educate the client in different methods of decision-making, so that the issues may be dealt with effectively. In so doing, you have to be careful not to be so counter-cultural as to be rejected.

A MOTIVATIONAL MODEL

At the beginning of this chapter, we noted that recommendations must be accepted by:

- those responsible for translating them into decisions;
- those responsible for translating them into action.

If the populations of these two groups are different, or overlap only partially, then the process of selling the recommendations has to be done to both. In both cases it is helpful to have a model of how people are motivated, to decide how to put across recommendations in a way calculated to be most attractive.

The motivational model that I use is shown in Figure 8.1 and is a type of path–goal model.

Typically, you want a client to take a *decision* (eg to accept a recommendation) or to take *action* (eg to implement a recommendation). The attractiveness of taking this step will depend on the outcome. The value of the outcome to you is that it will help you to achieve the assignment objectives. The value of the outcome to an individual will be as a pay-off.

Sometimes what appears to be rejection is a simple breakdown in communications: the client did not realise what was being asked. If what you are asking is clear, however, an individual's acceptance or rejection is dependent on:

- what *pay-offs* the outcome might have, and their desirability;

- the individual's *confidence* that taking the decision or action required will lead to these pay-offs (shown as factors A and B in the figure).

The desirability of the pay-off

Pay-offs have not only a rational but also an emotional component,

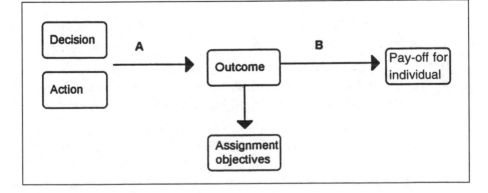

Figure 8.1 *A motivational model*

which is why people do not react wholly rationally to a proposal. Rational pay-offs will be assessed as benefits in respect of the individual's role at work – eg:

- Your department will perform better.

- Costs can be cut.

- You can do something you were unable to do before.

- This problem will be solved

The emotional pay-offs are different. What then, are the emotional pay-offs that drive people? Various breakdowns have been suggested, but set out below are four. (I am indebted to my colleague Ken Dietz for drawing this model to my attention.)

- security;

- belonging;

- recognition;

- creativity.

Going back to the ICC case study cited in Chapter 1 and elsewhere, suppose that John Smith had reached the conclusion that a total quality management (TQM) programme was required to reduce product costs. There are strong reasons for proceeding, but he has to consider the emotional pay-offs for the general manager (GM), who has to accept this recommendation. The method John Smith could use to appeal to each of the pay-offs is set out below:

- *Security* TQM is a well-established methodology. Launching a programme will address the issues and achieve the objectives safely and well.

- *Belonging* A TQM programme will involve all staff; the GM and his staff will be able to work together as a team on this project.

- *Recognition* Launching a high-profile TQM programme will demonstrate to head office that the GM is addressing the issues of product costs. With success may come the opportunity to advise other subsidiaries of the parent company on this.

- *Creativity* A TQM programme is new for ICC. Programmes can be tailored to suit the needs of each organisation, and the GM can take an active part in the design.

These pay-offs apply not only to the acceptance of recommendations, but also to the process by which recommendations are generated in the first place. For example, the GM's emotional pay-offs could be met while formulating recommendations, as follows:

- *Security* Kept regularly informed of progress, so that final recommendations come as no surprise.

- *Belonging* Being part of the steering group running the project.

- *Recognition* Naming some part of the implementation after the GM (eg if the GM's name is Stubbs, calling working groups considering TQM improvements 'Stubbs Groups').

- *Creativity* Allowing the GM to contribute ideas, and using these ideas.

Although everybody has these emotional needs, some will provide stronger drives than others; the aim should be to satisfy the strongest for the individual. And, as with needs generally, an unsatisfied need is a powerful motivator. The GM's needs will change according to circumstances. If – for example – his job is under threat, then security will rise to be the most powerful need.

Confidence building

Considering the desirability (or otherwise) of the pay-off in both rational and emotional terms is no more than a basic principle of persuasion. There is a good chance that consultants consider this implicitly, without explicit analysis. The approach above, however, can be helpful if confronted by an apparent failure in getting recommendations or their implementation accepted. More often, however, the difficulty lies in lack of confidence that the expected outcome or pay-offs will be achieved.

There are two important factors affecting confidence:

- The *clarity of the connections* between decision (or action) and outcome, and outcome and pay-off.

- The *expectation* that the decision or action will lead to the outcome, and the outcome to the pay-off.

To make the *connections* clear, it is important that the consultant engages in educating the workforce in the nature of the changes and the outcomes expected. The connections may not be as obvious to those affected as to the consultant and more senior management. As a rule, everybody is concerned about things that affect them, but their perception of what is relevant can vary widely. So the consultant may need to show how – for example – business benefits can be to the advantage of the individual employee.

This process of education has a pay-off, in that those people affected by a change are usually best placed to see how it might be implemented most effectively. This they can do if they are aware of its detailed nature.

The second factor affecting confidence – expectation – is more often the reason a change fails to be accepted. For example, if a stranger approached you in the street and asked for £1,000, saying that he could double it by investment in a period of one month, it is unlikely that you would give him the money. The pay-off is (I assume) desirable – with a guarantee of doubling your money in a month, you could borrow the money and still make a profit. The steps are clear to see – give the man £1,000, get £2,000 back in one month. The difficulty arises because you would not have the confidence that the stranger would actually double your money.

Likewise, people may clearly acknowledge the benefits of a particular course of action and understand the steps involved. But if their expectations of success are low, they will not take the action or decision required.

My early training was as a production consultant, applying work study and incentive schemes to improve employee productivity. We were told that on the introduction of an incentive scheme, people would often not even attempt to achieve the standard required (despite the rewards offered) because they did not believe they could achieve them. (A bit like trying to persuade a reluctant child to swim out of her depth for the first time.) A consultant has to engage in confidence-building methods that will encourage people to undertake change. Such activities may include:

- involving those affected at an early stage;

- breaking the change down into small steps, so that pay-offs can be achieved on completing each stage;

- visiting places where the change has already been successfully implemented;

- introducing the change on a pilot basis.

TRANSLATING RECOMMENDATIONS INTO ACTION

The challenges for a consultant in turning recommendations into action are:

- Getting recommendations accepted by those affected and gaining their commitment.

- Managing the change process.

- Ensuring that the client has an ongoing capability to support the change after implementation – ie that transfer takes place.

Gaining commitment

Although in theory it is possible to demand compliance with a change, positive commitment from those affected will yield better results. The following will help to build commitment.

- *Changes should be owned and supported by the client organisation* Any change should be seen as an initiative being taken by the client organisation, rather than being identified with the consultants. Active and visible support from top management is required. Giving the project a special name can also help (eg the TQM project for ICC cited earlier in this chapter might be entitled 'Project Silver').

- *Participation leads to commitment* People will be more committed if they are kept informed and participate in decisions. The sooner this starts, the better. It may not be possible to involve everybody from the start (eg before a decision has been made to proceed), but thereafter, involvement should be more than is usual. For example, although junior members of staff may not decide where their office is to be located, they might have a say in the layout and decor of where they work.

- More time and resources need to be allowed for communication during a change – existing communication arrangements may not be adequate by themselves. Similarly, there may need to be more participation in decision-making. A useful technique here is 'reservations in the right to decide'. Rather than delegating specific decisions to those affected by the change, define those that they should not make, and then leave the remaining decisions to them.

- *Honour resistance*   Resistance is the opposite of commitment, and dealing with it usually means overcoming it. Richard Beckhard, however, talks of 'honouring resistance' (Beckhard, 1989). This attaches a value to those who resist by assuming that they do so for what to them are sound reasons. These reasons could be germane to the success of the project, and ignoring them would be foolish. There will be some people, however, who cannot make the change and who therefore resist it irrationally. They may eventually have to transfer job or leave the organisation rather than impede the rest.

Managing the change process

Implementing change is a process, and it is a process that has to be managed. The previous section on gaining commitment implied that change often involves new ways of communicating and taking decisions. Key points in managing a change process are:

- *Allow sufficient resources for carrying out the change*   Not only does the substance of change take time, but so too does the process. There is rarely enough organisational slack to enable people to undertake a major change while continuing with their existing level of work. Some reallocation of tasks to allow those involved the time to carry out the change is necessary, as well as support from outside consultants.

- *Launch the change*   Running some sort of event to mark the start of the change process can raise its profile and start the unfreezing process. A training course, workshop, 'kick off' meeting or similar event can be used.

- *Work with key people* There will be key people on whom you should devote more time than the rest. You should identify who can make a major difference to the success or failure of the project (not everybody will) and spend a disproportionately large amount of time with them.

- *Nurse the change during the early stages* There are bound to be teething problems with any change, and so more support is required during the early stages when people are learning the new ways. When trying anything new, performance falls (eg when a baby starts to walk, it makes less progress than when it crawled). People will need reassurance that this is to be expected, and does not mean that the change has failed.

- *Give feedback and celebrate success* People need to know how they are doing; feedback is therefore particularly important during the change process. Celebrating major milestones marks the successful progress of change.

- *Make sure that psychological and material rewards do not act as a barrier to change* If a bonus scheme, or the basis of performance appraisal, or career progression, is oriented to the old arrangements, people will be inhibited from changing. You should therefore make sure that rewards are modified to be consistent with changed circumstances.

Transfer

Transfer is the process of making sure the client has an ongoing capability to support the change after the consultant has gone. Methods of effecting transfer include:

- providing training;
- writing manuals and programmes;
- establishing systems and procedures.

Key points are:

- *Transfer is part of the project* If consultant and other resources are not contracted for transfer, it won't happen. Transfer should be included, where appropriate, in the terms of reference and provisions should be made in the project costing for carrying it out.

- *Transfer should include follow-up*   Follow-up visits by the consultant can be used to ensure that transfer has been successful, and can be used to deal with any problems that might have cropped up.

A further advantage of follow-up is to consultants – it gives them a further right of entry to a client organisation, and therefore opportunity to sell further consultancy assignments.

9

MANAGING THE CLIENT RELATIONSHIP

The managing director of a small family company was recounting his experiences over the previous ten years with consultants.

'My father started the business and, like many entrepreneurs, was very resistant to advice. It was only when we were approaching bankruptcy that we got in our first consultant who saved us.

Since then, our experience has been mixed. One consultant produced a report on meeting BS5750, which was four times as thick as necessary. He simply duplicated what he'd done for his last client; it was a disaster. The next – an energy consultant – didn't tell us anything we didn't know already and failed to tell us some things we already knew.

We had some craft training done by an outsider; that went well. We also got a consultant in to help us introduce payment by cheque for all staff. Not only did he do this, but he also gave us a valuable report on our industrial relations.

Later, we had a consultant from a highly reputable firm to advise us on our marketing. We had some specific questions to which we particularly wanted answers. The consultant didn't bother answering our questions. The only impact he had on our business was one of creating annoyance.'

It takes so much effort to win clients, but very little to lose them. Selling has often been likened to courtship; but after the client has been won, the eagerly courted girlfriend can become a neglected wife, who complains, 'You never bring me flowers anymore.' In one instance, a consultant promised a proposal to a new director of a long-standing client. Owing to pressure of other work, the consultant forgot his promise and failed to submit the proposal (a situation unique in my experience!). The director was so incensed that he persuaded his colleagues not to use the consultancy on any further projects whatsoever. The relationship was ruined, and the client completely lost.

These examples illustrate the two key aspects of managing a client relationship:

- meeting the client's needs on a technical basis;

- providing a good standard of service.

It is this latter aspect about which this chapter is particularly concerned.

WHY THE CLIENT RELATIONSHIP IS IMPORTANT

A good client relationship yields considerably more benefits than simply the esteem of a satisfied client. Quite apart from the fact that it is easier – and more pleasant – to do business with a satisfied client, there are clear commercial advantages.

Strategic benefits

Products and services can be based on the spectrum shown in Figure 9.1. At one end you have unique products; a famous painting might fall into this category. Fairly close to that end must be the suppliers of a monopoly product. At the other end are commodity products – those that change very little according to the supplier, and for which there are many suppliers. Food retailing is an example of this: there is no difference in a particular brand of soap power according to the shop you buy it at.

Plainly a salesperson is in a much stronger position when a product lies towards the left-hand side of the spectrum. The purpose of branding a product is to move from the right-hand side towards the left, by giving attributes to the product additional to the qualities of the product itself. At the simplest level this might be attractive packaging; in the service industry it is achieved by reputation and fashion.

The services offered by a consultancy firm are often undifferentiated products; how the services are delivered is therefore fundamental in creating a good reputation. The quality of a consultant's reputation is vital in getting new business. Positive recommendations from satisfied clients to others in their network are worth many hours of selling and

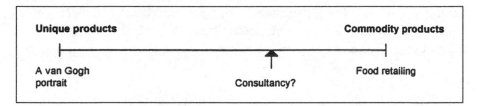

Figure 9.1 *A spectrum of products and services*

marketing by the consultant. Conversely, there is much truth in the old adage 'one bad job costs a hundred good ones'.

A good relationship helps sales

As has been already noted, former clients are perhaps the best source of further business – either by asking the consultant to continue to provide services in a particular area of specialisation, or by giving the consultancy practice the opportunity to provide a wider range of services.

Conversely, few consultants can claim to have an invulnerable client base. Just as they will seek to enlarge the size of their businesses by acquiring the clients of their competitors, so too will their competitors themselves be attempting to do the same. A poor client relationship will make a client more open to an approach from a competing consultancy practice for future work.

The client relationship must be actively managed

It is tempting to believe that the quality of client relationships is simply the result of luck or happenstance. This is not true. The client relationship must be actively managed in a way which is complementary to the technical work being carried out by the consultant. Consultants must bring competency to both these tasks if they are to be truly effective.

Consultants have taken up their specialisation because of their interest in the topic. Their training is directed towards achieving excellence in the technical aspects of their work. But the judgement made by clients about the quality of a consultant will not be simply on the technical aspects of their work together; it will also depend on a variety of other factors that contribute to the nature of their relationship. For example, the consultant who carries out a project to a high standard but takes too long over it will leave a trail of discontented clients.

Client relationships deteriorate rarely because consultants think them unimportant or are personally insensitive. It is that the task of active client relationship management can often too easily be crowded out by other activities until some (avoidable) crisis arises which brings it forcibly to the consultant's attention.

FACTORS CONTRIBUTING TO THE QUALITY OF A RELATIONSHIP

In this chapter we will be looking at client relationships in the context of a consultancy project. There will also, of course, be relationships with organisations for whom the consultancy is not currently working (eg past clients) or with joint venture partners.

Every consultancy project starts with a fund of goodwill from the client towards the consultant. There is no particular reason under normal circumstances why this should be exhausted during a project – except by mismanagement. What a consultant needs to know is the anatomy of client satisfaction (or dissatisfaction); this can be derived from an understanding of the client relationship.

The quality of a client relationship will depend on:

- features of the consultancy practice;

- characteristics of the client;

- the consultancy project being undertaken and its effect on the relationship.

Given an understanding of these, a consultant can plan and manage a client relationship so as to optimise it. The chapter therefore concludes with some suggestions concerning the skills and activities that will help to create satisfied clients.

Features of the consultancy practice

One reason that client relationships suffer is that there is a natural

Table 9.1 *The different wants of clients and consultancies*

Clients want:	Consultancies want:
The most appropriate consultant	To use who's available
Instant attention	To service a number of clients
To pay only for the time spent on the job	To bill as much time as possible
	To train inexperienced consultants
Experienced consultants	To spread experienced people thinly

conflict between the needs of a consultancy practice and those of its clients. These are set out in Table 9.1. This conflict becomes focused in the individual consultant, who is subject to demands from several sources. Consultants often have more than one client, each with their own requirements and seeking a level of service as if each was the only client. The consultant also has duties to his or her own employer and superiors. (See Figure 9.2.)

Taken together, these demands may present consultants with a dilemma; do they look after client A or client B first? Do they carry out the additional work that they know client C requires, or do they take on

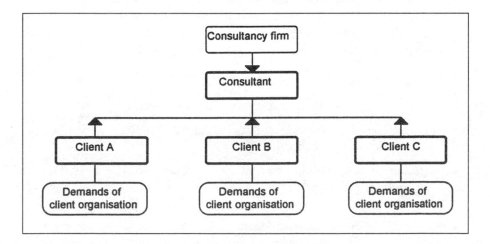

Figure 9.2

the more lucrative work of client D? Consultants will also have their own preferences in terms of the type of work they undertake or clients they deal with, which will also influence the choices they make.

The skill with which consultants can deal with these conflicting demands has a considerable influence over their ability to manage the client relationship.

Characteristics of the client

Not only does the consultant have a responsibility for the quality of a client relationship – the client also has a responsibility. This is not simply policing the services being provided by the consultant – it is active cooperation. The relationship between consultant and client should be a partnership, working together towards the same project goals.

The individual with whom the consultant is dealing will also be subject to demands, as shown in Figure 9.2. Sometimes these change, and in turn so too do his or her requirements of the consultant. The consultant must be sufficiently flexible to respond to these changes where necessary.

Another important consideration is how well the client uses consultants. Being an employer does not automatically make someone a good manager. Similarly, although the client is paying a fee, this does not make them expert at using consultants. What makes for a good client? Eve Bingham, writing in *Management Consultancy* magazine in April 1992, cited the following, based on her research:

Good clients bring to [the] relationship:

- a clear picture of desired results, but not how to achieve them;

- a tough, questioning approach to proposals, demanding to see how a course of action will deliver;

- a recognition of the importance of feedback, so the consultant constantly learns about results, positive or negative, of their interventions;

- an appreciation that it needs time to build a relationship by keeping in touch, taking time to explore the brief and encourage questions, to review feedback and to redesign the project if necessary;

- a sensitivity to the importance of acknowledging a positive contribution: the ability to say thank you.

Helping the client become a good client

Not all clients, sadly, exhibit these characteristics, so one of the tasks of consultants is to help their clients to become *good* clients. After all, if the client has never used consultants before, there is no reason why they should be able to use them well. And, even if they have used them, they may be misguided. So here are three, contradictory, precepts to remember in dealing with clients:

1. *The client is always wrong* The popular adage is, of course, 'the customer is always right'. This cannot – must not – be the case in consultancy, where the consultant's role is to take a view independent of the client. You should therefore question the assumptions, objectives and constraints set by clients and ask, 'Are these appropriate?'

2. *The client is often right* Having done the questioning above, the consultant will come to this conclusion, but there is more to this precept. Sometimes it can be easy as a consultant to develop a mind-set that clients are misguided incompetents, who can do nothing without the help of a consultant. So you need to be aware of the strengths of a client's thinking and decisions, as well as the weaknesses.

3. *Sell them what they need in terms of what they want* This phrase has been repeated often in this text, and it is repeated here. Occasionally there may be a need for confrontation, but the rest of the time – go with the flow. In this sense, dealing with clients is like the art of judo. In judo, skill lies not in opposing your opponent but in directing their energy so that they throw themselves. The art in dealing with clients is to direct their energies so that they move in the desired direction. A technique for doing this is to start in their preferred direction, but to educate them by use of data feedback so they start to look at things differently and move in a more appropriate direction.

The effect of the project on the client relationship

A consultancy project will affect the client relationship not just in terms of its technical quality, but also through:

- the quality of project performance;

- the quality of the personal relationship between client staff and consultant.

Figure 9.3 shows the key elements in each of these.

The quality of project performance

It is rarely the technical quality of a project that leads to client dissatisfaction; clients are more interested in ends than means. The key aspect of a project that influences a client relationship is therefore that of the *deliverables* – what the consultant is to provide to the client. It is for these that the client has engaged and will pay the consultant. The timing of deliverables is also crucial; clients get upset when deliverables are behind schedule.

Methods are the means used to create the deliverables. Problems arise with methods when there is disagreement about the details, or whether the consultant or client was meant to carry out a particular task. As we have also seen in Chapter 8, every consultant activity has an impact on the client system. Problems can also occur therefore when a project has an unwelcome effect on the client. It is a rare project that does not involve some client participation, so it is important to be clear about:

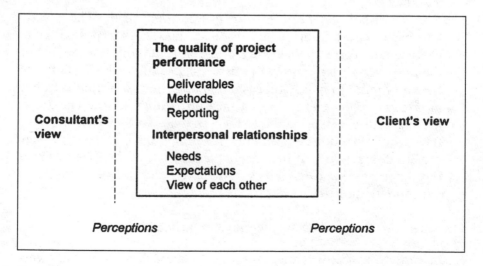

Figure 9.3

- who should be involved;

- how they should be involved.

The basis of *reporting* to the client should also be clear; clients become irritated when they do not feel adequately informed.

The quality of interpersonal relationships

As already mentioned, it is reasonable to assume that at the start of an assignment the consultant team begins with a fund of goodwill from the client. So the aim must be at least to avoid disappointing the client and, preferably, to improve the client's view of the consultants.

As the relationship is between individuals, the quality of the interpersonal relationship between the consultant and the client's staff will have an effect on the total relationship. The important factors are shown in Figure 9.3.

The needs of the client must be considered in terms of the project and how it is to contribute to the client's personal objectives. Problems occur if a consultant does not discern a client's real needs. Sometimes a client might have a hidden agenda, either as a principal or ancillary objective of the project. (Usually these agendas are political in nature!)

If clients' *expectations* are not met they will be disappointed and relationships will suffer. You must therefore take care to manage the client's expectations so that they can be met. These expectations relate not only to the project but also to you yourself – for instance, in the way in which you conduct yourself. For example, if you are working on client premises, the client may have firm expectations about:

- what time you should arrive and leave;

- whether you can use the telephone on business other than that to do with the project in hand;

- style of dress;

- your access to people in other departments or at more senior levels;

- the degree of formality in your relationship with client staff.

Infringing these expectations can have just as serious repercussions on the consultant–client relationship as failing to meet the formal terms of reference. Consequently, many consultants use the period of familiarisation at the start of an assignment to collect data on the 'code of conduct' they are to follow within the client organisation.

In a similar way, you can have quite legitimate expectations of a client. You can reasonably expect the client:

- to be accessible;

- to provide the resources promised;

- to cooperate in the execution of the project;

- to be supportive of the project;

- to tell you of changes of circumstances that may influence the project;

- to discuss any concerns or apprehensions about how the project is proceeding.

Although these are all the responsibilities of the client, you should check that they are being provided. If they are not, it is your job, as the expert, to alert the client to any difficulties and advise on how they should be resolved.

How the client and consultant view each other will depend on the other items already mentioned. That relationship will in part be a self-fulfilling prophecy; if the consultant loses the confidence of the client, for example, the client will become far more difficult to satisfy.

Occasionally you find that there is conflict between a client and a consultant, or between members of client staff. A good diagnostic rule in analysing conflict is to remember the sequence:

1. goals;
2. roles;
3. procedures;
4. personal animosity.

What this sequence suggests is that if you run into conflict, do *not* assume it is necessarily a matter of personal animosity – there are other probable causes, which are shown in the order of the list above. The easy way to remember the sequence is to imagine two people undertaking a car journey, who are arguing. They will argue if:

- they have not agreed on where they are going (goals);

- although they have agreed where they are going, they have not agreed who is to drive (roles);

- although they have agreed on where they are going and who is going to drive, they have not decided the route they are to take (procedures).

If, after agreement on all these points, they are still arguing, then perhaps it can be put down to personal animosity!

Perceptions are all

Figure 9.3 also illustrates that all the transactions between consultant and client are viewed through their respective perceptions. It is not 'objective reality' which matters, but how you each see things. The client's opinion will be affected by:

1. How he or she evaluates progress on the project compared with the promises you have made.
2. The impression the client has of the overall professionalism of the practice.

Item (1) above is about communications and expectations. A key job for a consultant in managing client relationships is to reassure the client that the project is proceeding satisfactorily. This means not only communicating progress, but ensuring that the client's expectations accord with those of the consultant. For example, returning to the ICC case study, John Smith may embark on a project to study alternative methods of producing cutlery. In so doing, he might choose to discuss the pros and cons of present methods with the operatives at ICC. If, however, the general manager's view is that there should be no consultation, there is a mismatch of expectations. Keeping the client informed is not just about reporting the past but also managing his or her expectations for the future.

The impression of the professionalism of a consultancy practice depends on the administrative as well as professional staff. The client comes into contact with switchboard and secretarial staff, receptionists, and with accounts people in respect of invoices. Most contacts will be fleeting and will not be face-to-face, but all will contribute to the client's impression of the practice. Many professional practices have therefore trained all their staff in key aspects in delivering good client care.

MONITORING THE CLIENT RELATIONSHIP

Remember clients will always have a view of the consultant, but whether they tell the consultant of their view is another matter. This is illustrated in Figure 9.4.

Note that there is on each side a threshold of dissatisfaction or satisfaction which must be reached before the client will comment on it. The consultant's aim must be continuing positive satisfaction, rather than simply assuming that no feedback means that the client is satisfied. There are two things that the consultant must do to address this:

- Monitor the quality of the client relationship by actively soliciting feedback.

- Adopt good practices in operating consultancy projects, so that the risk of client dissatisfaction is reduced.

Regular progress reviews enable the client to feed back concerns, and to be used to manage expectations. Even so, there is a danger that the consultant does not hear what the client is saying; you have to listen carefully to hear softly-voiced criticisms.

Handling complaints

Inevitably, from time to time a client may complain about progress or the way a job is being run, or the impact of it on client staff. Do not overreact to complaints – they might not be justified, or could be totally unfounded.

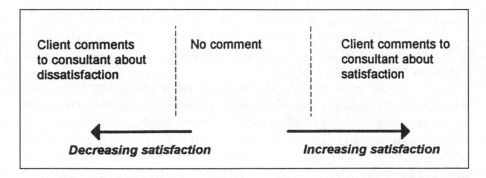

Figure 9.4 *The client's comments*

Here is an effective way of handling a complaint from a client.

- Thank them for having brought it to your notice and for giving you a chance to put it right. (Far better this way than that they should simply get annoyed, leaving the matter unresolved.) Tell them you're sorry they have been upset, but don't apologise for having done something wrong. (You don't know if it's your fault at this stage, but you can regret their being upset.)

- Encourage them to give you the full story and note the details. Don't interrupt while the client is giving vent to their feelings, and don't argue, however justified you think you may be in doing so. This will only make them more irritated.

- When you have got all the information, check whether the complaint is well-founded. Sometimes difficulties arise from misunderstandings, and a simple explanation will sort things out. If you cannot deal with the complaint at this meeting, however, explain this and tell the client what you plan to do. In particular, agree when you will get back to them with a response and make sure you do follow up.

A critical test of any provider of goods or services is how they handle complaints. If a complaint is handled professionally and well, it can strengthen rather than weaken the client relationship.

It is important to know when to call for help when dealing with a complaint. This is particularly necessary when a complaint is about you (when you are not in the best position to resolve it) or if the client is seeking some commercial compensation. Sometimes things do go wrong (no consultant is perfect), but do not compound the mistake by not asking for help when you need it.

CREATING SATISFIED CLIENTS

The comments thus far in this chapter have been somewhat defensive, focusing on how to avoid a poor client relationship. The remainder of this chapter looks at the other side of the coin – how to carry out consultancy projects so that clients are positively satisfied, rather than simply 'not dissatisfied'. This starts with the planning of the project, continues throughout the delivery, and finishes with its completion.

Setting up the project

Clear and comprehensive terms of reference and terms of business are the foundation of a good client relationship (see Chapter 5). If you did not sell the assignment, but are operating a project sold by someone else, then you should check that the points have been covered. If they have not, you must clarify them right at the start of the project:

- the scope of the project;

- the deliverables to the client;

- the method by which you will carry out the project;

- the programme of work involved;

- the resources required, including the support you expect from the client;

- the fees you are charging and when they become payable;

- when the project is to be complete.

You also need to know something of the sponsor, particularly their attitude to the project. What are the pay-offs for him or her if the project is successful – what will they get out of it? How accustomed are they to using outside advice? If a client has not used consultants before, they may need help in using your services to best effect.

Planning the project

With any project other than the most trivial, it will be necessary to have review or reporting points with the client during the project. Progress reviews might take place at a regular frequency (eg once per week or per month) or at milestones – points in the project where a major phase or stage is complete.

Progress reviews can do much to reassure a client that a project is proceeding well and build confidence in the consultant. The converse – not keeping a client informed – can result in their feeling out of control or vulnerable, even if there is no basis for this.

When making your project plan, try to build in some slack so that you have some flexibility to accommodate delays. If your planning is such that any change in circumstances means that you will fail to meet targets, inevitably this will happen.

During the project

There are several things you can do which will enable you to develop a good client relationship during a project:

- *Build confidence during the early stages*   Every project should start well – after all, you would not have won the contract if the client did not have the confidence that you were the best firm for the job. But during the early stages, even established clients will be checking out the firm's credentials, to see if that first impression was correct. Early in a project it is particularly important, therefore, to build a client's confidence. Being prompt and prepared at all client meetings – perhaps having them more frequently than you might otherwise have – will help; as will a business-like approach and achieving all the initial targets required on time. One particularly good way of building confidence at the early stages is the 'quick success' – achieving a result or delivering value beyond that expected.

- *Add value*   The 'quick success' formula will work throughout a project, so try to add value by doing more than the client expects. This does *not* mean providing free services, but look for opportunities of giving extra benefits from your work, or help that may be beyond your brief. The most commercially advantageous ways to you are those which are valuable to a client but cheap for you to provide. A simple example is giving a client a publication or report from the consultancy practice on a topic of concern to him or her.

- *Publicise good news*   Make sure the client knows about all the successes you have achieved in your project. This can be done via progress reviews, but also make sure you can bring them up during casual conversations with client staff. If you are really sophisticated you will plan 'sound bites' so that you have a snappy response to the query 'how is it going?' Your sound bite should consist of a newsworthy comment about how the project is going. These items can be passed on by client staff. Remember that your client will be wanting to reassure his or her colleagues that the project is proceeding successfully.

- *Dealing with bad news*   If something goes wrong which can be easily remedied without concerning the client, then there is no need to bother him or her. If the client has to be informed, then it is better to do so before the problem becomes a crisis. Ideally you should go to the client with a statement of the problem and how you propose to solve it. Sometimes, however, you may need to work together to resolve the problem. Often clients will put in extra effort to solve the problem or mitigate its effect on their organisation to save their own credibility with their colleagues.

The end of the project

I am told that in one European country there is the phrase, 'To say goodbye like an Englishman' – which means to go without saying goodbye!

The best source of further work and referrals to new clients is past clients, and so every project should be concluded with this in mind. The project should be signed off from both sides – the consultancy's and the client's. There should be clear agreement on the successful completion of the project, and an exchange of letters confirming the client's satisfaction. Astute consultants will make sure that warm letters of praise from clients are passed on to their own superiors.

Personal skills of the consultant

There are skills that make it easier for consultants to manage client relationships well. They are as follows:

Managing your time effectively

Time is the consultant's stock-in-trade; it is the commodity which you are selling. Time is also a consultant's scarcest resource, so it must be managed carefully. This requires three important skills:

- establishing and working to a set of priorities;
- giving sufficient time to existing commitments;

- learning to say 'no'. Contrary to popular belief, there are a limited number of hours per day that a consultant can work at optimal performance. There comes a point when a consultant has to say 'No' to the demands of a practice or the client.

Positioning yourself correctly

A consultant must position him- or herself so that they are the equal of the client – at whatever level the client is in the organisation. In particular, the consultant should make clear the right to say 'no' to a client, for example when they have unreasonable fee or timescale expectations.

Handling 'no-win'

It may not be within the consultant's power to resolve a conflict of demands between a client and the consultancy practice. This is particularly difficult for junior consultants, who could find themselves in a 'no-win' situation – they will upset someone whatever they do. They should seek the help of a more senior consultant – their boss – to resolve it.

When things go wrong, deal with them

Inevitably there will be occasions when things go wrong at either the project or personal level between consultant and client. When this happens, it should be recognised as a problem and dealt with as such. It is the way a consultant deals with problems which is a key test of how good he or she is at managing the client relationship. Young consultants are frequently reluctant to admit to mistakes which they cannot deal with; far better to admit to them, however, before they turn into crises.

Not knocking anybody

It rarely redounds to a consultant's credit to criticise his colleagues, his clients or his competitors to his client. Where a client has a justifiable complaint about a consultant colleague, the consultant should acknowledge and deal with it, rather than denigrating his colleague.

Being attentive

A lot of effort goes into wooing the client for business. Once the business has been secured, the client will still expect attentive service. In practice this means that the consultant must be accessible to his clients and give them prompt attention. Equally, the consultant must be able to avoid the 'time-wasters' without losing them as clients.

A final benefit of a good client relationship

Although in this chapter I have dwelt on differences between consultants and clients, there is much to unite us – not least the improvement of the client's business. In this respect, the consultant and client staff are colleagues, albeit in different organisations.

For me, one of the joys of consultancy is the rich variety of colleagues from my clients that I meet and work with. I commend it!

REFERENCES

Beckhard, R (1989) 'A model for the executive management of transformational change', *The 1989 Annual: Developing Human Resources*, University Associates.

Bennett, R (1990) *Choosing and Using Management Consultants*, Kogan Page, London.

Bingham, E (1992) 'It takes Two to Tango', *Management Consultancy*, April.

Cowell, D (1984) *The Marketing of Services*, Heinemann Professional Publishing.

Handy, C (1989) *The Age of Unreason*, Business Books.

Kotter, J P (1978) *Organizational Dynamics − Diagnosis and Intervention*, Addison-Wesley, Wokingham.

Majaro, S (1988) *The Creative Gap*, Longman, Harbour.

Markham, C (1991) *Practical Management Consultancy*, Accountancy Books, London (first published as *Practical Consulting* in 1987).

Miller, R B and Heiman, S E (1989) *Strategic selling*, Kogan Page, London.

von Oech, R (1990) *A Whack on the Side of the Head*, Thorsons, London.

Schein, E H (1988) *Process Consultation*, vols I and II, Addison-Wesley, Wokingham.

Wittreich, W J (1966) 'How to Buy/Sell Professional Services', *Harvard Business Review*, March/April.

The Institute of Management Consultants has published two documents jointly with the Management Consultancies Association on quality assurance in consultancy practices; they are:

The Top Consultant

- *Guidelines for Management Consultancy*
- *Practice Notes for Management Consultancy*

APPENDIX 1
GUIDELINES FROM THE INSTITUTE OF MANAGEMENT CONSULTANTS CONCERNING SELLING AND PROMOTING CONSULTANCY SERVICES

GENERAL OBLIGATIONS

Members are free to promote their practice in any way which appears appropriate, provided always that they observe the following obligations towards their colleagues, clients, the Institute and the Profession.

1. The manner of the promotion is ethical, dignified, accurate and designed not to mislead.
2. No disrepute is brought on the Profession or any member of it.
3. The tenor of the promotional activity is that of informing rather than soliciting.
4. The services promoted are within the competence of the member's practice.
5. Clients are identified only if their specific authority to do so has been given.

Methods of promotion

Members may employ appropriate methods of promotion including media advertising (newspapers, magazines, radio, TV, teletext), lecturing, seminars, exhibitions, PR (press releases and articles) and sponsorship of academic or public interest events provided the general and other obligations above are followed and subject to the following additional guidelines:

- Direct mail: mail shots should always be addressed to named individuals.

- Cold calling and canvassing: visits to prospects should be by appointment.

- Entertaining and gifts: entertaining should be reasonable in scale and any gifts of modest value.

- Arrangements for introductory fees to agents, including other consultants are acceptable. However, financial or other substantial considerations should not be given to clients or their staff or any other given person who may influence a decision to employ consultants.

- Events sponsored must be of a nature consistent with the ethics and dignity of the Institute and the Profession.

APPENDIX 2
CONDITIONS OF CONTRACT
APPLYING TO A PROPOSAL

This appendix contains the conditions of contract that were at one stage recommended by the Institute of Management Consultants for use by its members. In view of the variety of work now carried out by management consultants, the Institute no longer provides sample conditions of contract. These are included here as an indication of the points that might be included in a consultant's terms of business.

The conditions set out below have been approved by the Institute of Management Consultants. Detailed terms and any variations to these Conditions agreed with the client are contained in the Proposal.

1. Definitions

'The Client' means the person, firm or company so named in the Proposal.

'The Consultant' means the person firm or company contracting with the client for the provision of management consultancy services and includes, where the context permits, any employee of the Consultant.

'The Proposal' means the offer in writing by the Consultant to undertake the Assignment.

'The Assignment' means the management consultancy services to be provided by the Consultant to the Client in accordance with the Proposal.

'The Contract' means the agreement between the Client and the Consultant consisting of the Proposal, the Client's written acceptance of the Proposal, and these Conditions.

2. Application of conditions

Except where inconsistent with the express written terms of any contract between the Consultant and the Client, these conditions shall apply to all contracts for management consultancy services between the Consultant and the Client.

3. Formation of contract

No binding contract for the performance of the Assignment will come into existence until the Consultant has received the Client's written acceptance of the Proposal.

4. Fees

(a) General

Fees as detailed in the Proposal are charged under the Contract for time spent by the Consultant in performing the Assignment, including travelling time, whether at the Client's premises or elsewhere. No charge will be made for time during the Assignment period represented by illness or voluntary absence of the Consultant, but no reduction is made for public, national or statutory holidays.

(b) Overseas Assignment

Fees and expenses will be paid by the Client in the currency and at the place shown in the Proposal.

Fees for an overseas Assignment of up to four weeks' duration are payable in advance. If the Assignment is of a longer duration, the Fee quoted in the Proposal will be paid as to one-third in advance of the commencement of the Assignment, one-third at the halfway stage of the Assignment and one-third on completion of the Assignment.

5. Expenses

(a) General

Travel, subsistence and out-of-pocket expenses directly related to the assignment are charged at cost unless an overall fee to include such expenses is agreed with the client and recorded in the Proposal.

(b) Overseas assignments

(i)   Travel and subsistence costs
Prior to any travel overseas by the consultant on the Client's business, the Client shall pay or advance, agreed travel and subsistence costs as set out in the Proposal.

The Consultant's travel and accommodation arrangements overseas will be made by the Client. Surface travel and accommodation will be at the first-class rate, short-haul air fares will be at the tourist rate and long-haul air fares at the first-class rate.

(ii)   Travel documents and work permits
The Consultant will use his best endeavours to provide himself with all necessary visas and travel permits but the Client undertakes to assist as necessary. The Client is responsible for arranging Work Permits where necessary.

6.   Value Added Tax

VAT, where applicable, at the current rate will be added to the Consultant's Invoices.

7.   Payment

The Consultant will invoice the Client in accordance with the Proposal. Invoices are payable in full forthwith upon receipt.

8.   Fee rates

The Consultant reserves the right to increase the fee rates shown in the Proposal to take account of inflation. The Consultant will give the Client three months' notice of any increase in fee rates applicable to an uncompleted Assignment.

9.   Termination of assignment

The Assignment may be terminated by either party giving the other two weeks notice in writing. On termination, the Consultant will invoice the Client for work done and expenses incurred up to the end of the notice period.

10. Forecasts, etc by the consultant

The time taken to complete the work and the measure of its success depend in part on factors outside the control of the Consultant. These include the degree of cooperation given by the Client's staff and promptness in agreeing and implementing recommendations. Any forecast or estimate made by the consultant of the time required for the assignment and the results attainable is given in good faith having regard to the information made available by the Client and represents the Consultant's interpretations of the Client's instructions. Any such estimates and any confirmation or variation of them in subsequent reports and correspondence shall not be deemed in any circumstances to be undertakings, warranties or contractual conditions.

11. Office and secretarial facilities

The Client will make available suitable office and secretarial facilities for the Consultant throughout the period of the Assignment.

12. Additional work

Any variation or extension of the work done by the Consultant not covered by the Proposal, is not part of the Contract and will be the subject of separate arrangements with the Client and confirmed in writing.

13. Code of professional conduct

As a member of the Institute of Management Consultants, the Consultant has given an understanding to abide by the Institute's Code of Professional Conduct ('The Code'). The full text of the Code is shown in [Appendix 3]. The Client will note that the Code requires that the Consultant will not disclose or permit disclosure of or use to his own advantage any confidential information concerning the Client's business without the Client's written permission. The Code also required the Consultant to disclose any interest he may have in a business which is in competition with or supplying goods or services to the Client.

14. Arbitration

All disputes, differences on questions at any time arising between the Client and the consultant in relation to or in connection with these conditions and all contracts between the Client and the Consultant shall be referred to the arbitration of a person to be mutually agreed upon or failing agreement of some person to be appointed by the President for the time being of the Institute of Management Consultants. The arbitration shall be in accordance with the Arbitration Act 1950 or any statutory modification or re-enactment thereof for the time being in force.

APPENDIX 3
CODE OF PROFESSIONAL CONDUCT

The following principles are reproduced from the Institute of Management Consultant's Code of Professional Conduct:

PRINCIPLE 1

High standards of service to the client

A member shall carry out the duties which he has undertaken diligently, conscientiously and with due regard to his client's interest.

Rules

1.1 A member will only accept an engagement for which he is suitably qualified.

1.2 Before accepting an assignment, a member shall clearly define the terms and conditions of the assignment including the scope, nature and period of the service to be provided, the allocation of responsibilities and the basis for remuneration. (See Notes **1.2.1** and **1.2.2**)

1.3 A member will regard his client's requirements and interests as paramount at all times.

1.4 A member shall only sub-contract work with the prior agreement of the client. (See Note **1.4.1**)

1.5 A member will hold as strictly confidential all information concerning the affairs of a client unless such information has been released for public use, or specific permission has been given for its disclosure.

1.6 A member will refrain from inviting any employee of a client advised by the member to consider alternative employment; (an advertisement in the press is not considered to be an invitation to any particular person).

1.7 A member will develop recommendations specifically for the solution of each client's problems; such solutions shall be realistic and practicable and clearly understandable by the client.

1.8 To ensure efficient performance of each assignment, a member will exercise good management through careful planning, frequent progress reviews and effective controls.

Notes

1.2.1 Before undertaking or continuing with any work, a member should ensure that his resources are adequate and properly directed to carry it out.

1.2.2 The terms of an assignment should always be evidenced in writing.

1.4.1 When sub-contractors are employed, the principal consultant will take responsibility for the quality of the work produced and for compliance with the requirements of the Code. Members are referred to the Institute's Guidelines on Subcontracting Agreements.

PRINCIPLE 2

Independence, Objectivity, Integrity

A member shall avoid any action or situation inconsistent with his professional obligations or which in any way might be seen to impair his integrity.

Rules

2.1 A member will maintain a fully independent position with the client at all times, making certain that advice and recommendations are based upon thorough impartial consideration of all pertinent facts and circumstances and on opinions developed from reliable relevant experience.

2.2 A member will declare at the earliest opportunity any special relationships, circumstances or business interests which might influence or impair his judgement or objectivity on a particular assignment. (See Notes **2.2.1**, **2.2.2** and **2.2.3**)

2.3 A member shall not serve a client under terms or conditions which might impair his independence, objectivity or integrity; he will reserve the right to withdraw if conditions, beyond his control, develop to interfere with the successful conduct of the assignment. He will not practise during a period when his judgement is or might be impaired through any cause.

2.4 A member shall not take discounts, commissions or gifts as an inducement to show favour to any person or body.

2.5 A member will advise the client of any significant reservations he may have about the client's expectation of benefits from an engagement. He will not accept an engagement in which he cannot serve the client effectively.

2.6 A member will not indicate any short-term benefits at the expense of the long-term welfare of the client, without advising the client of the implications.

2.7 A member will not discuss and agree with the client any significant changes in the objectives, scope, approach, anticipated benefits or other aspects of the engagement which might arise during the course of carrying it out.

2.8 A member who, in circumstances not specifically covered in these Rules, finds that his professional or personal interests conflict so as to risk a breach of this Principle shall, as the circumstances may require, either withdraw from the situation, or remove the source of conflict, or declare it and obtain in writing the agreement of the parties concerned to the continuance of his assignment. (See Note **2.8.1**)

Notes

2.2.1   Rule 2.2 requires the prior disclosure of all relevant personal, financial or other business interests which could not be inferred from the description of the services offered. In particular this relates to:

- any directorship or controlling interest in any business in competition with the client;

- any financial interest in goods or services recommended or supplied to the client;

- any personal relationship with any individual in the client's employ;

- any personal investment in the client organisation or in its parent or any subsidiary companies.

2.2.2   A member shall not use any confidential information about a client's affairs, elicited during the course of his assignment, for his own personal benefit or for the benefit of others outside the client organisation. There shall be no insider dealing or trading as legally defined or understood.

2.2.3   If any such business or financial interest arises during the course of an assignment, Rule 2.8 shall apply.

2.8.1   It should be noted that the Institute of Management Consultants may, depending on the circumstances, be one of the 'parties concerned'. For example, if a member is under pressure to act in a way which would bring him into non-compliance with the Code of Professional Conduct, in addition to any other declaration which it might be appropriate to make, he should declare the facts to the Institute.

PRINCIPLE 3

Responsibility to the profession

A member shall at all times conduct himself in a manner which will enhance the standing and public regard of the profession.

Rules

3.1   A member recognises that he has a responsibility to the profession, as well as to himself and his clients, to ensure that his knowledge and skills are kept up to date, and will take appropriate action to this end.

3.2 A member will not knowingly, without permission, use copyright material, or a client's proprietary data, or materials or techniques that others have developed but have not released for public use.

3.3 A member shall have a proper regard for the professional obligations and qualifications of those from whom he receives or to whom he gives authority, responsibility or employment, or with whom he is professionally associated. (See Notes **3.3.1** and **3.3.2**)

3.4 A member shall only initiate or accept a joint assignment with a member of another professional body if he is satisfied (and can satisfy the client and if required, the Institute) that such an assignment would be conducted to the standards represented by this Code of Professional Conduct.

3.5 A member referring a client to another management consultant will not misrepresent the qualifications of the other management consultant, nor will he make any commitments for the other management consultant.

3.6 A member will not accept an assignment for a client knowing that another management consultant is serving the client in a similar capacity unless he is assured, and can satisfy himself, that any potential conflict between the two assignments is recognised by, and has the consent of, the client. (See Note **3.6.1**)

3.7 When asked by a client to review the work of another professional, a member will exercise the objectivity, integrity and sensitivity required in all technical and advisory conclusions communicated to the client.

3.8 A member will negotiate agreements and charges for professional services only in a manner approved as ethical and professional by the Institute. (See Note **3.8.1**)

3.9 A member shall not attempt to obtain work by giving financial inducements to clients or client staff. (See Note **3.9.1.**)

3.10 A member, in publicising his work or making representations to a client, shall ensure that the information given:

- is factual and relevant;
- is neither misleading nor unfair to others;

- is not otherwise discreditable to the profession.
  (See Note **3.10.1**)

Notes

3.3.1   Under Rule **3.3**, a member will provide all possible opportunities for management consultants he employs to exercise their professional skills as widely as possible within the interests of the client, and will, as opportunities arise, assist them to accept progressively greater responsibility in accordance with their ability and experience.

3.3.2   In a similar way a member will encourage the management consultants he employs to maintain and advance their competence by participating in continuing professional development.

3.6.1   Legal and 'fair trading' obligations should take precedence in both public and private sector work.

3.8.1   Members are referred to the Institute's 'Guidelines on Charging for Management Consulting Services'.

3.9.1   Payment for legitimate marketing activity may be made, and national laws and customs should be respected.

3.10.1   Accepted methods of making his experience and/or availability known include:

- publication of his work (with the consent of the client);

- direct approaches to potential clients;

- entries in any relevant directory;

- advertisements (in printed publication, or on radio or television);

- public speaking engagements.

Members are referred to the Institute's 'Guidelines on the Promotion of Management Consulting Services'.

Index